City Quilts

12 Dramatic Projects Inspired by Urban Views

Cherri House

stashBOOKS

an imprint of C&T Publishing

Text copyright © 2010 by Cherri House

Artwork copyright © 2010 by C&T Publishing, Inc.

Publisher: Amy Marson

Creative Director: Gailen Runge

Acquisitions Editor: Susanne Woods

Editor: Cynthia Bix

Technical Editor: Susan Nelsen

Copyeditor/Proofreader: Wordfirm Inc.

Design Direction: Kristy Zacharias

Cover/Book Designer: Kerry Graham

Production Coordinators: Jenny Leicester and Kirstie L. Pettersen

Production Editor: Alice Mace Nakanishi

Illustrator: Rose Sheifer

Photography by Christina Carty-Francis and Diane Pedersen of C&T Publishing, Inc., unless otherwise noted.

Published by StashBooks, an imprint of C&T Publishing, Inc., P.O. Box 1456, Lafayette, CA 94549

Library of Congress Cataloging-in-Publication Data

House, Cherri.

City quilts : 12 dramatic projects inspired by urban views / Cherri House.

p. cm.

ISBN 978-1-57120-847-7 (softcover)

1. Patchwork--Patterns. 2. Quilting--Patterns. 3. City and town life in art. I. Title.

TT835.H66 2010

746.46'041--dc22

2009038057

Printed in China

10 9 8 7 6 5 4 3 2

DEDICATION

To Luke, Elizabeth, Ashlee, Melissa, and Mom—thank you for always believing in me!

To Rich—thank you for your encouragement and support.

ACKNOWLEDGMENTS

A special thank you to my editor, Cynthia Bix, for your kind guidance.

Thank you C&T for this wonderful opportunity!

Thank you to Robert Kaufman Fabrics for all of these wonderful solid fabrics in these glorious colors!

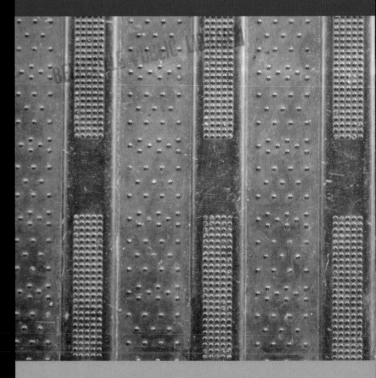

Special thanks to Houston Metropolitan Research Center, Houston Public Library, Houston, Texas, for permission to reprint the historical city map of Houston on page 7.

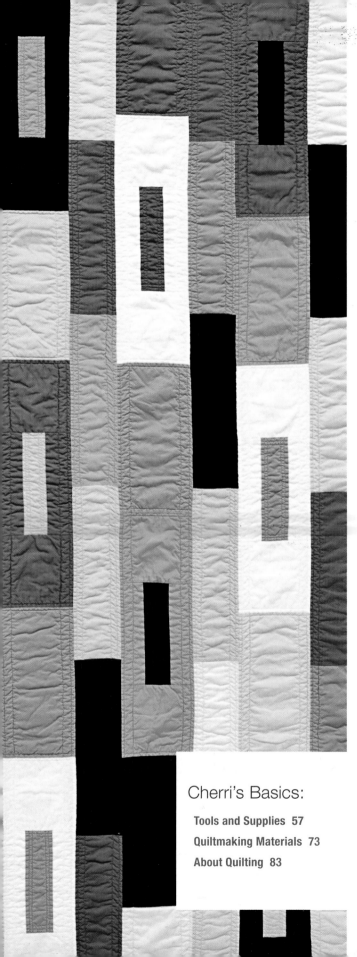

Contents

Cherri's Basics:

Urban Inspirations

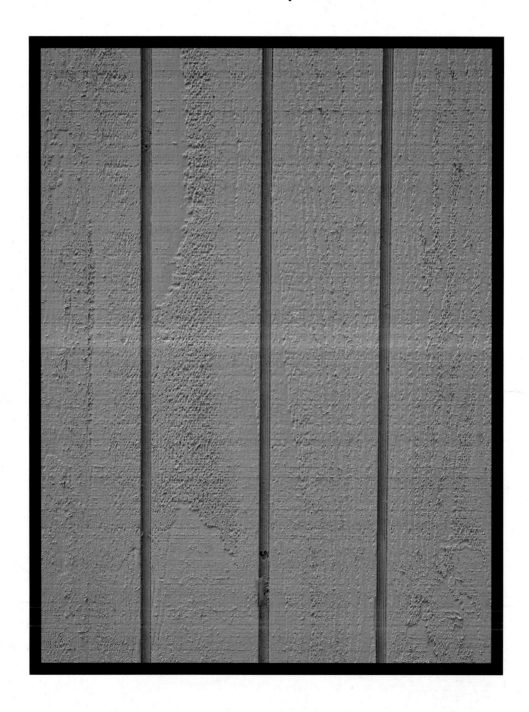

The quilts in this book, inspired by the patterns and textures of the city, are simple, graphic, and geometric—glorified utility quilts, if you will. They're the kinds of quilts that your grandmother might have made if she had had a treasure trove of solid fabrics. I'm not a fan of the saying "These aren't your grandmother's quilts." Some of the most amazing quilts I've seen were made by someone's grandma. Utility quilts, Amish quilts, maverick quilts, scrap quilts, quirky vintage quilts—many are artistic treasures. Even those that missed the mark were still a labor of love.

You will find no elaborate Baltimore Album quilts in this book. I'm not sure if I have what it takes to make one of those heirloom beauties that seem to take a lifetime to create. These City Quilts are meant to be kindly used up, to be loved, to be appreciated, and to be given freely. When I think of something being used to its fullest, I think of Margery Williams's children's book *The Velveteen Rabbit,* about the stuffed toy rabbit that is made "real" through being loved. That's the life I want for the quilts I make. Whether they warm your heart, your home, your bed, or your loved ones, as I tell my friends, "It's all about the love, baby." These are the quilts of my heart. Aside from my children, this is the best I have to give. I hope you, too, will find joy in making, using, and giving these quilts.

WHY CITY QUILTS?

Houston skyscraper

I love cities, big and small, and I especially love downtowns. One of my favorite pastimes is walking in cities, from the downtowns of Boise, Salt Lake City, Los Angeles, Chicago, and New York to those of Rome and London. The adventure of walking in a new city is like unwrapping a present. Funky little restaurants, corner grocery stores, city parks, fountains, and theaters—you get their true flavor when you explore them on foot. And best of all, you can meet new people in their unique cities.

In Houston, my city, one of my favorite treasures is downtown with its amazing high-rises, tiny churches, parks, outdoor sculptures, festivals, theaters, restaurants, and something we all

appreciate—the Houston International Quilt Festival! I work in downtown Houston in a high-rise office building. Every day I drive to work early in the morning, when the lights of all the buildings glow before the sun rises. No matter how many times I see those lights, they fill me with joy! I love the high-rises with their varied windows, building shapes, and heights. Everywhere there are fascinating patterns—in the pavings, on walls and gates, in shop windows, in the city parks.

The quilts in this book are a reflection of my city home. Inspirations for seven of them—the buildings, parks, and shops—were gathered from about a ten-mile radius.

The quilt designs in this book are simple and geometric, like the architecture and the layout of the city. The pleasing shapes of squares and rectangles are a backdrop for compositions that are created using color, light, texture, balance, and movement.

Though simple in piecing and technique, City Quilts are about the whole, and not the parts. Many of the quilts in this book are composed of a single, repeated square or rectangle, but this shape becomes secondary to the overall design achieved through color placement, value, and the mood of the piece. Through variation of color and value, squares of fabric can become panes in a window, or an aerial view of a parking lot or a city park. (For more about color and value, see page 23.)

Their simplicity makes them beginner-friendly. If you have basic sewing skills and some under-standing of simple quiltmaking, you will find that the construction is very straightforward—no complicated shapes to sew together, just straight seams. If you need a little additional skill-building information to help you complete the projects, refer to Quiltmaking Essentials (page 103).

If you are a more experienced quilter, these designs offer a fresh, modern aesthetic and an opportunity to play with color using all-solid fabrics.

ON THE GRID

Cities have long been planned and built along grids—square grids, sometimes with diagonal lines crossing them, and even concentric rings. Just as cities are built on grids, all of the quilts in this book are based on grids—mostly on squares and rectangles, and sometimes on half-square triangles. Though simple, their beauty is classic and timeless. Cities grow; with a well-planned foundation the possibilities are immense.

City of Houston map from 1836

With the skills mastered through the making of these quilts, you will build a foundation of limitless possibilities for further exploration and discovery of your own quilting style.

The gridded arrangement of blocks is the foundation of a traditional patchwork quilt. Simple or complex, the symmetrical organization of the selected components is key to all the decisions that will follow. Once you gain mastery of the construction process in terms of fabric preparation, seam allowances, and block construction, creating any gridded quilt you desire is within your reach. Here's an exercise in seeing a quilt in a grid: Find a simple grid—windows in the wall of a skyscraper, a pattern on a floor, anything you can find. Identify the key elements, and recreate the grid on graph paper.

The windows of a skyscraper become the quilt blocks, and the supports become the sashing. You determine the width and height of the blocks; you determine the width of the sashing. The freedom to design is available to anyone who takes the time to understand the components, the structure, and the construction of a quilt.

Blocks and sashing in *City Lights* echo grid of skyscraper windows (full quilt on page 43).

The blocks for most of the quilts in this book are sewn together in a *straight set*—arranged in horizontal rows with block edges parallel to the sides of the quilt (for example, *City Bank,* page 65). Exceptions are *City Center* (page 53) and *City Circle* (page 59), which are arranged in a *diagonal,* or *on-point, set.* Two options for quilts set on the diagonal are to either slice off half of the outer blocks to have a clean edge, as in *City Fair* (page 23), or add setting triangles, as in *City Center* and *City Circle.*

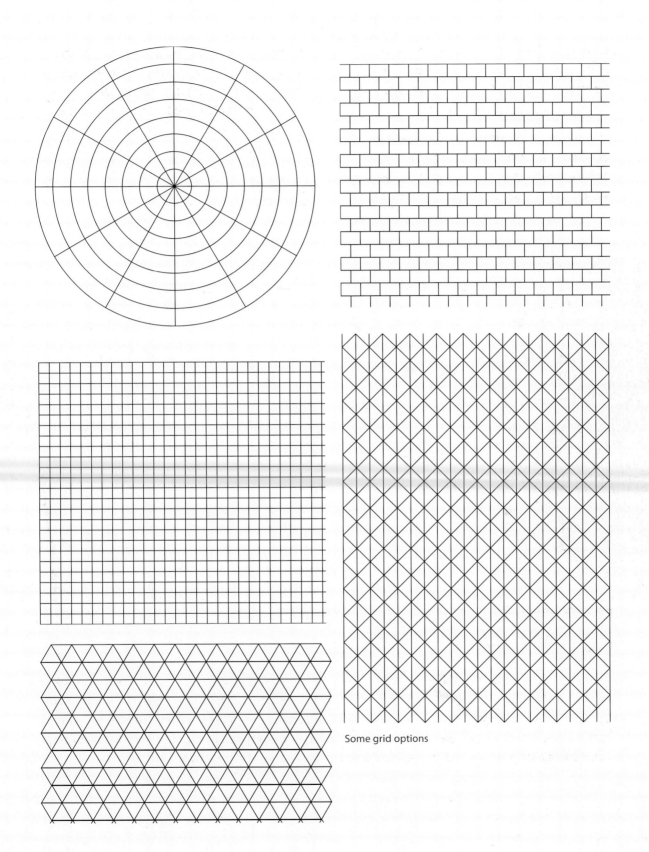

Some grid options

Quilt blocks, city blocks

The structure of many quilts is a grid of *blocks*. A block may be a single piece of fabric or a pieced block made up of individual units or patches of fabric sewn together. It can be a simple Four Patch block made up of four smaller squares, or it might have 36 individual patches or more. (Relax—there are none of those in this book!)

The blocks may or may not be joined with *sashing*—kind of like sidewalks in the city. Sometimes called *lattice,* sashing can be strips of fabric, pieced or not, that join the blocks. Sashing is often used to frame or to give distinction to a block, but it's not necessary or recommended for every quilt. The width of the sashing should be balanced with the size of the block. Too wide, and it could overwhelm a small block—too narrow, and it could be lost among large blocks.

Sometimes there are *cornerstones*—little squares at the corners of the blocks where the sashing strips meet.

Borders are the fabric frame that surrounds the quilt top, almost like the streets that divide city blocks. They can be pieced or not. The quilts in this book have simple, squared borders (page 108). Again, borders are optional—not every quilt needs one. Whether or not your quilt has a border, it will need a *binding*—the narrow, folded fabric strip that forms the finished edge of the quilt.

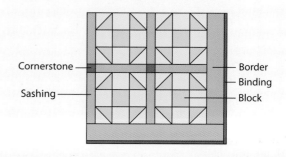

Cornerstone ——

Sashing ——

—— Border
—— Binding
—— Block

CONTEMPORARY OR TRADITIONAL? A LITTLE OF BOTH

Several of the quilts in this book, such as *City Center* (page 53) and *City Play* (page 99), are based on traditional quilt blocks such as Log Cabin, Four Patch, and Nine Patch. These old favorites are based on squares and rectangles. Others, such as *City Aviation* (page 47), feature blocks like Flying Geese, which are based on half-square triangles. Several other quilts in the book, such as *City Tracks* (page 69), *City Harbor* (page 79), and *City Lot* (page 85), are original patterns. But even they are based on squares and rectangles, like the traditional blocks.

Log Cabin block from *City Center*   Classic Log Cabin block

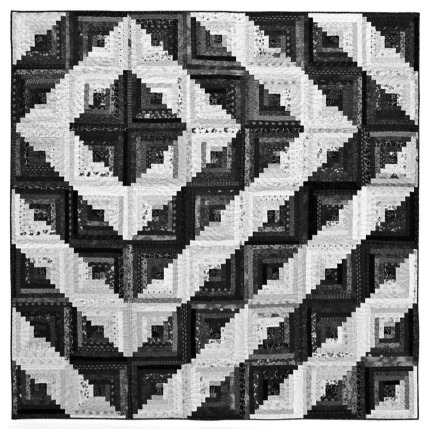

Elizabeth, 75˝ × 75˝, made by Cherri House and machine quilted by DeLoa Jones, uses traditional Log Cabin blocks in a traditional barn raising setting but looks contemporary because of its asymmetrical design.

When I envision the marriage of traditional and contemporary, I think of Amish quilts, which are certainly traditional but still look fresh and current. Amish quilts have been such a source of inspiration to me. The makers combined solid colors in limited palettes with simple blocks and incredible quilting to create masterpieces that are timeless classics.

Other perfect examples of the fusion of traditional and contemporary are the now-famous Gee's Bend quilts—quilts with a bold, graphic style created by the self-taught women of this tiny southern town. Traditionally made from cast-off clothing and other salvaged fabrics, these quilts incorporate prints as well as solid fabrics. Yet they still have that distinctive geometric look. Gee's Bend quilts displayed in museums are often grouped by the traditional pattern that was the starting point for the quilt. One example, the House Top series, features quilts based on the Log Cabin block, but the makers' unique interpretations leave tradition far behind. (To find out more about Amish and Gee's Bend quilts, see Resources, page 110.)

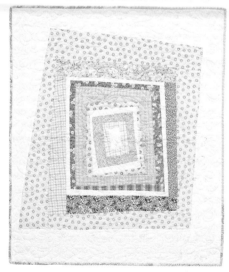

Little House, 30˝ × 36˝, made and machine quilted by Cherri House

This is my interpretation of a Gee's Bend House Top Quilt.

What's old is cool again!

Notice the craze over cooking, gardening, paper arts, knitting, crocheting, embroidery, sewing, and quilting? It seems there is an explosion of interest in home arts. There is something so satisfying about creating with our hands. I believe we need to create, to give, and to share with those we love and with those in need. We are nurturers, and through these arts, we nurture.

When I was small, I asked my mother if she was a house-wife, and she said, "No, I am a homemaker. I'm not married to a house—I'm making a home." All of these arts and skills make our homes and our world a better, kinder place to be.

Today there is a huge interest in these arts, and they have an ever-expanding presence on the Internet through blogs, websites, groups, and forums. Maybe the more technical and computerized our world becomes, the more we need simple, down-to-earth comforts. We have the best of both worlds: We go to books and the Internet for instructions, inspiration, and support, and then turn off the computer to create something with our hands.

Making a traditional pattern contemporary

Following are some suggestions to keep in mind when you want to update simple traditional blocks to create a more unique, modern quilt.

Use a minimalist approach to fabric selection. The blocks in *City Aviation* are as traditional as they come. But by limiting the palette to relatively few neutrals and inserting several plain blocks into the quilt top, I was able to give the quilt a contemporary minimalist look. The star of the show is the quilting, which mimics the blocks and echoes the shapes. *City Aviation* is very understated; you must look closely to take in all that there is to see.

 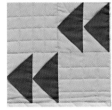 

Traditional blocks—Pinwheel (left), Flying Geese (center), and Four Patch (right)—have an updated look in *City Aviation* (full quilt on page 47).

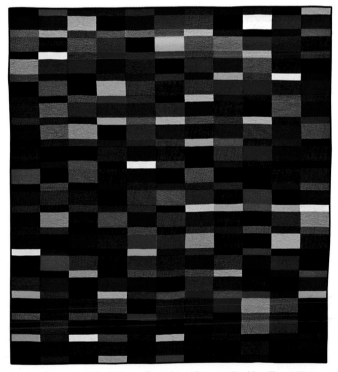

Foreign Currency, 61″ × 68″, made and machine quilted by Cherri House

Throw in something unexpected or quirky. Try a shock of color—something different. The "something quirky" can be subtle: a bit of humor, a piece of fabric that relates to the name of the quilt or to the recipient—anything that will make the quilt personal. Those personal touches help break your quilt out of the traditional mold. My quilt *Foreign Currency* (page 12) is based on the very traditional quilt design called Chinese Coins, which features bars of fabric separated by sashing; hence the name. This quilt has shocking little bits of bright orange tossed in all over the quilt. There are very few of them, but they pull you in and keep your eyes bouncing from block to block.

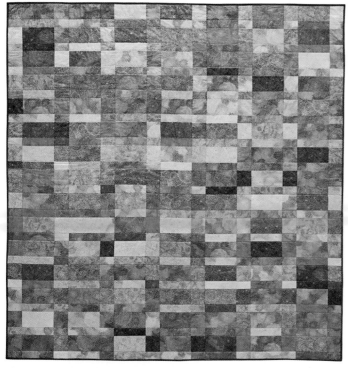

Florin, 63″ × 67″, made and machine quilted by Cherri House
This simple design lets the fabrics shine.

Let fabric do the work for you. Whether you choose solids or printed fabrics, when you carefully pair the right fabric to the right quilt pattern, much of the design work is done for you. There is no need to "reinvent the wheel"—if a fabric is glorious in its entirety, find a way to utilize it. The fabric in *Florin* was so beautiful that it didn't need to be cut up into little pieces, framed, or embellished in any way. It only needed the chance to shine. There is nothing complicated about this quilt, but the individual parts become secondary to the overall effect. Let the fabric work for you!

Blocks in *City Play* are traditional Nine Patch blocks put together with a new twist (full quilt on page 99).

Select simple blocks with a minimal number of pieces. Become a detective when looking at quilt blocks, and analyze what can be simplified. *City Play* is a perfect example. It's a classic Nine Patch quilt with sashing and cornerstones. But by making the sashings in different colors and different lengths, the cornerstones and sashing have effectively disappeared and have become floating frames around the Nine Patch blocks.

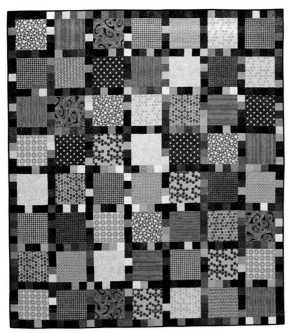

City Blocks, 70″ × 80″, made and machine quilted by Cherri House

Make a big statement with bold color choices. *City Blocks* is a riot of color. Some colors are spicy, some subtle—but the variety keeps you hopping. This quilt was inspired by the idea of neighborhoods and how they vary from block to block. The occasional pops of white are a sharper note than any of the bright colors—they are the attention seekers in this quilt. Think in terms of themes, moods, locales, and flavors. Want a spicy flavor? Use hot colors like red, orange, fuchsia, and yellow. Do you want the coolness of the ocean? Use a variety of blues and greens.

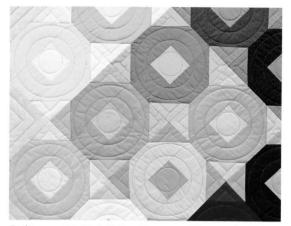

Quilting on *City Circle* (full quilt on page 59)

Use quilting to contribute to the overall effect you want to achieve. Will the quilting be utilitarian (to hold the quilt together) or star of the show? For example, in *City Circle* I wanted an emphasis on circles, and this was added with the quilting. In *City News,* I used a clear monofilament thread on the black-and-white fabrics to create straight lines like the type in a newspaper, and in contrast the "red-all-over" background has heavy all-over quilting. *Cherry Fizz* is a traditional Log Cabin quilt made from floral fabrics, but with the bold linear quilting, the quilt takes on a more contemporary feel.

For more about quilting, see Cherri's Basics: About Quilting (page 83).

The cumulative results of the pattern, fabric, and quilting choices that you make throughout the planning process will produce a quilt that is graphic, contemporary, and uniquely you!

Quilting on *City News* (full quilt on page 26)

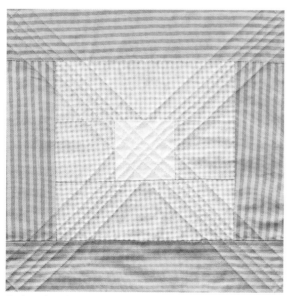

Quilting on *Cherry Fizz* (full quilt on page 25)

FABRIC:
The Joy of Solids

As you peruse the images in this book, my love of solid fabrics will quickly become evident. These are my favorite fabrics to work with, and creating these quilts has been a joy! But I didn't always like solids.

When I first started buying fabric for quilts, I was all about the marbled, fossil-fern, mottled look. Once, when I was fabric shopping with my mother, she asked if I was interested in the solids. I said dismissively, "Solids? No, I would never buy them—they're boring and flat." What an uneducated goof I was! Then, at the Houston International Quilt Festival, I saw an exhibit of incredible antique Amish quilts. It was truly an *aha!* moment. I don't remember how long I stood there staring at those beautiful old quilts. One in particular captured my attention—it was

black, purple, and blue, and it absolutely glowed I knew that my quilts were going to change because of what I was seeing. I was both determined to figure out how to work with solids and humbled because of my ignorance.

You too will see what wonderful effects you can create with cotton solids. These fabrics will never go out of style. They have withstood the test of time, and they are in a class of their own.

FABRIC SHOPPING

Readily available at quilt shops, 100% cotton solids are considerably less expensive than their printed counterparts. I advise you to purchase high-quality, high-thread-count, solid fabrics manufactured for use in quilting. Don't skimp and don't cut corners when it comes to fabrics! My favorites are Kona Cotton Solids by Robert Kaufman, available in more than 200 colors (see Resources, page 110).

Cotton versus polyester blends

Some quilters will use only use 100% cotton fabric, while others will use whatever works best for their projects, in terms of color, weight, and so forth.

Here are a few thoughts about the use of cotton fabric versus poly/cotton fabric in quilting:

- Most high-quality quilting cottons are similar in weight, whereas poly/cotton blends or synthetics can vary in weight, which will cause fabric stability issues in your quilt over time.

- Poly/cotton blends are less likely to wrinkle. However, 100% cotton holds a crease, which is great for finger pressing and pressing with an iron.

- For hand quilting, 100% cotton is easiest to quilt through.

- Cotton frays less than synthetic fibers.

- Cotton can be pressed on very high heat, whereas polyester can melt.

At the end of the day, it is a matter of personal preference. Are you making an heirloom quilt that you want to last for generations? If so, I'd stick with 100% cotton of the very best quality. Are you making a quilt for charity? Then I say, use what you have available, so you can get it made with a minimum of fuss and into the hands of someone who needs it and will gain comfort and enjoyment from it.

How much to buy?

Unlike printed fabrics, where a multitude of colors appears in a single yard, solids are in the "what you see is what you get" category. Working with solids often requires combining lots of different colors to achieve the look you want. To really take advantage of the rainbow of colors available in solids, you'll want to build up a wide-ranging stash. For example, in a quilt like *City Play* (page 99) I used more than 60 individual colors. Some quilts will require a large quantity of one particular color but only a small square of another. Many of the quilts in this book use the same colors numerous times.

My recommendation is to build a collection of 100% cotton solids in a variety of colors in ½- to 1-yard increments. By creating a palette you will be able to add variety and depth in terms of color and value to your quilts. How to start? Begin with a color family, a portion of the color wheel, or colors for a specific quilt. Wherever you choose to begin, having a varied selection of available colors will increase the richness and depth of your work.

Keeping a fabric record

I take fabric swatches taped to an index card with me when I shop to help me make fabric choices. When my quilt is finished, I add these cards and swatches to my quilt journal.

A QUILTER'S PALETTE

With the hundreds of colors available in cotton solids, you can achieve a very painterly effect in your fabric creations. Whether you are a contemporary, traditional, or art quilter, solids can be successfully incorporated into any quilt.

Understanding color

Do you have a color wheel? This handy, easy-to-understand visual illustration of color relationships is an essential tool for quilters. You can buy one at art stores and at most quilt stores. You can also draw and color your own, a great exercise in understanding color better.

The color wheel shows the three primary colors (red, yellow, and blue) placed equidistant from each other. Between them are the three

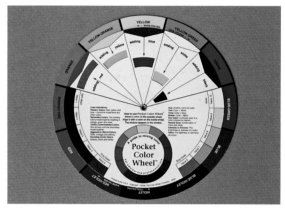

Color wheel

secondary colors (orange, green, and violet) and the six intermediary colors (yellow-orange, red-orange, red-violet, blue-violet, blue-green, and yellow-green), all of which are created by combining the primary colors. Neutral colors (black, white, and gray) are not part of the color wheel.

Fabric Preparation

To wash or not to wash? For the most part, I'm not a prewasher. Take into consideration the fabric that you are using. Are you familiar with the manufacturer? Have you used their fabric previously without problems? If you are uncertain about the fabric, and living dangerously is not your style, err on the side of caution by prewashing. I *do* always prewash hand-dyed fabrics and batiks because they are more likely to bleed.

Shout Color Catcher

Shout Color Catcher is a great product that I always use when I wash my quilts. These amazing little sheets, available at most grocery and discount stores, absorb excess dye in the wash water. When I wash a quilt, I throw in two or three sheets. The sheets generally come out lightly colored, and the quilts do not.

Color schemes

A *monochromatic* color scheme features a *color family*—a single color in all its tints, tones, and shades (page 21), varying from light to dark. Color value will be the key to keeping a monochromatic quilt fresh and interesting.

Monochromatic neutrals

A *complementary* color scheme pairs colors that are directly across from each other on the color wheel. A perfect example is red and green—the "Christmas colors." And how about purple and yellow, the colors of an iris? As always, nature is the best teacher!

Complementary colors of reds and greens

An *analogous* color scheme is any three colors that are side by side on the twelve-color wheel. Imagine an evening sky in shades of blue, blue-violet, and violet, or a sunset display of yellow-orange, orange, and red-orange.

Analogous colors of violets, blue-violets, and blues

A *triadic* color scheme is three colors equally spaced around the color wheel. The most basic is the popular choice for children's rooms—the primary colors of red, yellow, and blue. Or you could just as easily combine blue-green, yellow-orange, and red-violet.

Triadic colors of reds, yellows, and blues

A *cool* color scheme takes its colors from the "cool" half of the color wheel—the blues, greens, and violets.

Cool colors of blues, greens, and violets

A *warm* color scheme uses colors from the "warm" half of the color wheel—the reds, oranges, and yellows. *City Tracks* (page 69) is a good example of a warm-color quilt.

Warm colors of reds, oranges, and yellows

City Park, 72½″ × 77½″,
made and machine quilted
by Cherri House

This quilt is based on a cool color scheme.

Tints, shades, and tones

A *tint* is a color with white added to it. The pastels in *City Lights*
(page 43) and *City Sweets* (page 91) are good examples.

Tints used in *City Sweets*

A *shade* is a color with black added to it. The blue fabrics in *City Harbor* (page 79) are blackened shades.

Shades used in *City Harbor*

A *tone* is a color with gray added to it. *City Shops* (page 95) features grayed colors.

Tones used in *City Shops*

No matter what color scheme you select, it is essential that you use a variety of lights, mediums, and darks to create visual interest and movement. For example, *City Aviation* (page 47) is comprised of neutral fabrics that vary from almost white to a dark chocolate brown.

Fabrics used in *City Aviation*

The balance of color in a quilt must be finely tuned. Sometimes only a single spark of color is necessary to achieve the particular effect you are after. In *City Fair*, for example, there is one pale peach block, used to add warmth. More than one block would have diminished the effect of the color. In this way, fabrics function much like paint. You can add sparkle, light, and interest through your color selections.

City Fair, 62˝ × 66˝, made and machine quilted by Cherri House
Pale peach block in center left of quilt adds warmth and brightness.

Color values can be varied within a single block or across the entire surface of a quilt. In *City Fair*, the fabrics were placed in such a way as to create the effect of lights in the distance.

The importance of color value

Value in color simply means how light or dark it is. Its importance cannot be underestimated in creating a quilt that is alive with light, depth, and movement. This is true whether you're working with solids or printed fabric. In order to create an effective variance in value, the colors must crescendo and decrescendo in incremental steps from the starting color.

A fabric can be deceptive when viewed by itself; often the true color won't be visible unless it is placed next to other fabrics. The 3-in-1 Color Tool, available from C&T Publishing, has small green and red value finders, which are extremely helpful in determining the true value contrast between fabrics.

3-in-1 Color Tool with value finder

Selecting color for your quilt

Can you ever have too many colors in one quilt? Yes, probably, but I'll push the limit every time. I love color … the more the better. If ten greens make a great quilt, then wouldn't 30 greens make a better quilt? Be brave and push the color envelope where possible. Pick your main color, and then set your limits as far as you are able to go on either side of this on the color wheel. If your main color is red, extend your color selections to orange on one side and purple to the other, and use everything in between. Your compositions will have much more depth and variety by making these additions to your color selections. The differences from color to color are subtle, but the overall effect is great!

If you come from a traditional quilting background, your fabric selection process may begin with choosing your focus fabric and then gathering the supporting players. You will find that a different mind-set may be necessary when working with solids. Instead of a focus fabric, you may have a focus color or theme.

Background fabrics play an important role in many of the quilts in this book. Although they are considered neutral elements in most quilts, they are really the foundation for the entire piece. They determine how all of the colors play together, and they give the quilt its tone.

In *City Lot* (page 85), the background color is a chocolate brown, which sets off all the bright colors and gives the quilt a warm, playful feel. The white background on *City Sweets* (page 91) adds to the innocence and sweetness of the piece. *City Center* (page 53) has a predominately black background, but to break up the seriousness of so much black, I slipped in a few navy triangles for variety.

City Center background mixes black and navy blue (project on page 53).

Color inspirations

There is an endless supply of inspiration for color. If you have anxieties about choosing colors, here are some tried-and-true sources.

Nature is the best teacher, always and forever! Take a walk and really look at the colors around you. Notice all the colors in the sky at different times of the day. Look at a tree and count how many greens you see. Or look for all the shades of blue in a lake or stream. A comment I sometimes hear about my enthusiastic use of color is, "But it won't go together—the colors won't work." I say that if it works in nature, it will work in a quilt!

Master artists—such as impressionists Renoir, Monet, Van Gogh, and Seurat—were masters of color. You can't go wrong by using the colors in your favorite works of art for inspiration.

Advertisements and packaging can be a great source for color ideas. Companies spend big bucks getting the colors right for their marketing tools. Look at billboards and product packaging. Flip through the pages of a glossy magazine and take note of the colors used in the ads.

Creating a mood with color

Color and emotions are closely tied; the emotions associated with colors vary from person to person and from culture to culture. I was showing one of my daughters a quilt I was working on, and she didn't like it because it made her feel "cold." The quilt had very few colors, and none of them were warm.

Yellow quilts make me feel warm, white quilts make me think of weddings, and pink quilts make me happy. I've yet to encounter someone coming in contact with a baby quilt created in soft pinks and blues without uttering an audible "ohh!" Choosing colors based on their emotional impact is another approach to creating a unique and personal work of art.

Cherry Fizz, 43″ × 43″, made and machine quilted by Cherri House

A happy pink quilt!

SPECIAL EFFECTS

With careful choices and placement of color in your quilts, you can create special effects and illusions.

Create a "glow"

To create quilts that glow with light and color, you must have enough value and contrast in your fabrics to build intensity. If your fabrics are too "matchy," your quilt will be dull. I learned that the hard way when I chose fabrics to make a star quilt. I found a black print with tiny mauve and pale blue flowers and little mint-green leaves—at the time I thought it was beautiful. I found some *perfectly* matched fabrics in mauve, pale blue, and mint green to make the stars. After cutting out hundreds of squares of fabric and constructing way too many blocks, I started to assemble the top, and it was just awful! How could this fabric that was so perfectly matched fall so completely flat?

Then I learned how *gradations* of color can create a glow. Gradations are a series of step-by-step changes in color value, building in intensity in small increments. Gradations can be in a single color family or in a multitude of colors. Sorting colors into gradations by value is easier with solids, or near-solids, than with printed fabrics. Getting the idea of gradations was a *eureka!* moment for me. I knew what I needed to do to fix my quilt, and what to do for future quilts.

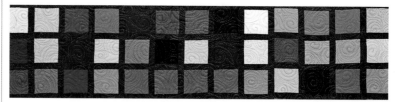

Color gradations in *City Green* (full quilt on page 75). Gradations of green look as parks and city lawns might look from an airplane.

The illusion of transparency

One of my favorite tricks is creating "transparency" using solid fabrics. Through your choice of fabric colors and layout, you can create the effect of two pieces of colored sheer overlapping to create a third color. The illusion of transparency is achieved by careful placement of the relative values of neighboring fabrics. In *City News,* for example, placing bow-tie blocks with darker value red fabrics and grayed black-and-white fabrics next to lighter value blocks creates the illusion of sheer areas—the illusion that there is another layer under the dark areas.

An entire quilt of the same color value would just be a two-color quilt. The magic only happens because of the relationship between neighboring colors.

City News, 70˝ × 70˝, made and machine quilted by Cherri House

City Circle also plays with the effect of over/under colors in relation to the values in the adjacent colors.

Detail of *City Circle* (full quilt on page 59)

Value and contrast can also be effectively used to create the effect of sunlight and shadow as well as layers.

In *City Play,* subtle but distinctive value differences make this block appear to be lit from behind (full quilt on page 99).

BACKING FABRICS

In many of my quilts, I like to add a playful note by choosing a print fabric for the backing. It can be a fun contrast to the solids on the quilt top, as well as an additional layer to the quilt as a whole. In a sense, it is the last page of the book—and the end should be as good as the beginning. The quilt back can be a reflection of the quilt top in terms of color or shapes. For *City Lights,* I selected the backing fabric because, in an abstract way, the pattern echoes the shapes of the building "windows" in the quilt top. For *City Harbor,* I thought the batik looked like deep water, which fit perfectly with the quilt's watery theme. Let your choice for your backing fabric be a thoughtful bonus to the quilt you have worked so lovingly to create!

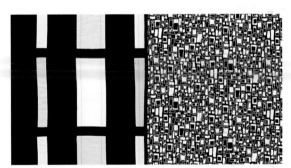

City Lights (page 43) has a geometric print backing.

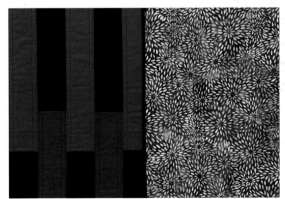

The blue batik backing on *City Harbor* (page 79) is the color of deep water.

DESIGN PLAY: Endless Possibilities

Patterns can serve different purposes for different people. For some, they are a road map to be followed to the letter. For others, they are general guidelines and a jumping-off point for their own creations, much like experimenting with a recipe. If you are in the latter category, the patterns in this book can serve as a launching pad for your own unique designs. Take these simple patterns, and build on them.

Mastering the skills to make the quilts in this book will open the door to designing your own creations. Change the dimensions of the blocks, change the width of the sashing (or get rid of it), change the layout—change whatever you want. Want a bigger quilt? Add more blocks. You are the designer and the creator of your own masterpiece. Understanding the fundamentals of quilt construction gives you freedom to do or create whatever you choose.

You can play with design using quilt design software on your computer or using good old graph paper and pencils.

DESIGNING WITH COMPUTER SOFTWARE

One of the best opportunities for seeing the possibilities in a quilt design is to use quilting software. The software will allow you to change multiple components within the quilt before you buy or cut into your precious fabric. In *City Green* (page 75), for example, I knew that I wanted to achieve the dappled look of sun and shadow beneath the trees. I tried multiple settings and configurations before deciding on the final look. I'll walk you through my steps, the choices that I made, and why. Often, options aren't a matter of good or bad—they can just be based on your personal preference or on your objective for the quilt's final look.

Quilting software is excellent for this kind of design exploration illustrated below, as well as for configuring yardage and cutting instructions. The software also enables you to add or subtract rows and columns in the quilt layout to create a quilt in any size you want.

I do EQ! ■ ■ ■ ■

I should have a tattoo that says: I ♥ EQ6! There are several types of quilt design software on the market, but The Electric Quilt Company program EQ6 is the one I use and am most familiar with (see Resources, page 110). It is a lifesaver for working out color choices, block layout, borders, yardage, and so forth. EQ6 is user-friendly, with great tutorials and videos. The company also has a wonderful support staff who never seem to tire of my phone calls and questions.

First option
I just didn't like this—the sashing was too heavy, and it made the quilt feel too dark.

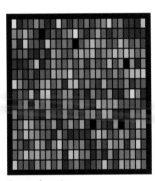

Second option
Here, I completely changed the sashing, reduced it in width, and elongated the block. I really liked this one, but it was too similar to *City Sweets* (page 91) in structure.

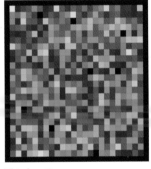

Third option
In this version, the sashing is removed entirely, causing the colors to all melt together. I love this design, and I will probably make it into a quilt sometime. But in the end, I wanted a narrow sashing to give the effect of a stained-glass window.

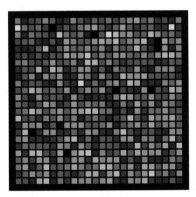

Final quilt: *City Green.* This is the quilt that I made (see page 75 for full instructions).

That all-important ¼ inch

Whether you design on the computer or on graph paper when determining the cutting measurements, don't forget to add in ¼-inch seam allowances!

DESIGNING ON GRAPH PAPER

If quilt software is not an option for you, graph paper and colored pencils work wonders. Graph paper is readily available in office supply and art supply stores. It's also available free on the Internet. Just search "free graph paper," select the paper you want, print it—and you're in business! I recommend 4 or 8 squares to the inch for designing. Decide on a scale you are most comfortable with, such as 1 square = 1 inch, and begin designing.

HERE ARE A FEW RECOMMENDATIONS:

- Begin by creating a quilt outline, minus any color.

- Make multiple photocopies in order to experiment with color. Use colored pencils to create multiple quilt configurations of units, blocks, and sashing.

- Pin the paper quilts on a wall, and look at them from across a room to create, in essence, a thumbnail sketch. This will help you get a better vision of what the finished quilt would look like.

- If you are working on the layout of a quilt, make multiple copies of the original concept.

- Cut out the small paper pieces—the units and blocks—and create several quilts on plain pieces of paper to visualize various quilt layout options. This cut-and-paste method may sound somewhat archaic, but I find this method enjoyable and even therapeutic.

Keep graph paper with you all the time for those sudden inspirations. Moleskine puts out little graph paper notebooks that are wonderful. I can't count the quilts that I've designed while sitting in church, in an airplane, even in traffic (not recommended).

Use whatever medium is best for you, whether it be software or graph paper; the most important part is capturing the inspiration and creating from it.

QUILT BORDERS

I'm not a member of the "every quilt needs a border" club. If a quilt has a border, it should be a part of the overall design and never an afterthought or something added to make a quilt larger. I think that quilts without borders tend to have a more contemporary feel.

Think of a border as a frame. Will the frame add to or detract from the composition? In *Rich Crackers*, a narrow inner border was needed to contain all of the color and movement within the quilt. The wider, off-white outer border creates a sense of calm for a busy quilt.

A narrow border was all that was necessary to frame *City Shops* (page 95). The border did need to be a color, not the predominant black and white. The deep blue softens what would otherwise have been a very stark quilt. In *City Circle* (page 59), a two-color border was created from setting triangles. The two colors emphasize the lights and darks within the quilt.

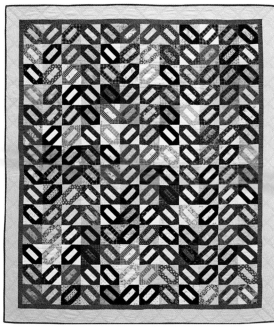

Rich Crackers, 56″ × 64″, made and machine quilted by Cherri House

Design wall

I cannot emphasize strongly enough the importance of a design wall for laying out your quilts. Because these quilts are about the whole and not the parts, you will need to be able to step back to view the quilt as you construct it.

A design wall need not be an expensive, renovate-your-studio kind of venture. You can simply buy an inexpensive tablecloth—the kind with a plastic surface and a flannel back. (Depending on its size and the size of the quilt you want to make, you may need two.) Hang up the tablecloth, flannel side out, on a wall, using thumbtacks or a staple gun. Another simple option is to hang up large pieces of batting, which can be cut from a roll at your local discount fabric store.

If wall space is not an option, lay your quilt on a floor. But make sure to do so in an area where you can get some distance and perspective, and, of course, where there isn't lots of foot traffic!

You can add a single border to a quilt or multiple borders of varying widths. Some quilts have a narrow inner border as well as a wider outer border. The widths of the borders should be proportional to the quilt top. As a general rule, I wouldn't make the border wider than the blocks in the quilt. For example, if the blocks are 6″ × 6″ finished, the width of the border should be 6″ or less. Wide borders give you an opportunity to add interesting quilting patterns such as grids or decorative motifs such as feathers. For narrow inner borders, I limit the size to 1″–1½″. For these borders, it's often effective to repeat a color you have used in the quilt blocks.

Quilts to give

Often we make quilts to give to someone. As you plan your design, ask: Where will the quilt live? Who is the recipient? Gather information before you get started. If you are making the quilt for someone else, conducting a bit of an interview will be very helpful. Do you know their favorite colors? Is their style over-the-top or subdued, ornate or plain? Regardless of the quilt pattern you select, this kind of knowledge will help you to create a very personalized, one-of-a-kind quilt.

City Center has both a narrow inner and a wider outer border (full quilt on page 53).

Like other design decisions, adding a border or not is a matter of personal preference. Before making any final decisions, put your quilt top on a design wall, and audition several different colors, fabrics, and width options.

QUILTING AS A DESIGN ELEMENT

Quilting is a design element, just like color and pattern, and it should ideally work in harmony with your entire quilt. Of course, it also has a practical function of holding the quilt top, batting, and backing "sandwich" together.

When you are deciding how to quilt your creation, consider the fabric, the style of the quilt, and the complexity of the blocks, as well as how the quilt will be used. For example, a quilt made for a three-year-old child needs sturdy quilting that will stand up to lots of use, whereas the quilting on a wallhanging can be mainly decorative. If you are new to quilting or unsure of the best solution, consult with an expert professional quilter about options suitable for your quilt. Your local quilt shop can also be an excellent resource for recommendations and suggestions on how to quilt your quilt.

Here, I'll walk you through the various kinds of machine quilting to consider from a design standpoint. All of them can be done on a domestic sewing machine as well as by a quilting professional. For basic information about machine quilting and the specialized machine feet needed, see Cherri's Basics: About Quilting, page 83.

Utility quilting

Often called quilting "in-the-ditch," this is a purely functional way to hold the quilt sandwich together. This quilting is done by stitching very close to the seamlines. The quilting is minimal, not decorative, and it is often all that is needed for a contemporary-style quilt where you want the colors and pieced shapes to be the focus of the quilt. This type of quilting can also be used to hold all the layers in place before adding more heavily quilted designs.

Straight-line quilting

Linear-quilted lines can add a strong design element to a contemporary-style quilt. With the use of a walking foot (page 83), straight lines can easily be achieved on a domestic sewing machine. Depending on the width of your walking foot, you can stitch straight, parallel lines at ¼˝ and ½˝ intervals by using the edge of the foot. Walking feet usually have an adjustable guide bar for quilting additional straight lines or creating grids.

Straight-line quilting on *City Aviation* (full quilt on page 47)

Tip

INCHIE RULER TAPE—adhesive measuring strips available from C&T Publishing—works perfectly for marking quilting lines. The tape sticks to your fabric during the quilting process, and it can be repositioned and reused (see Resources, page 110).

Free-motion quilting

Free-motion quilting adds a whole dimension of design and texture to your quilt. It can be done on a domestic sewing machine using a free-motion foot or a darning foot, with the feed dogs dropped (page 83). You can do overall or motif quilting with this method.

Overall quilting is a repeated shape stitched over the entire surface of the quilt. The shape can be a series of swirls, loops, circles, and more. The shapes can be loosely or tightly spaced, but they need to be consistent across the quilt.

Overall quilting on *City Play* (full quilt on page 99)

Heavy overall quilting on *City Shops* (full quilt on page 95)

Motif quilting can be any specialized design—hearts, airplanes, flowers, birds—anything you can think of that relates to the fabric, the theme of the quilt, the recipient, the block. I quilted a loose flower motif on *City Sweets* to mimic swirled icing on petit fours.

Quilted flower motif on *City Sweets* (full quilt on page 91)

Dive into free-motion quilting ■ ■ ■ ■ ■ ■

Many quilters are afraid to dip their toes into this particular pool, but don't be! It takes practice, but once you achieve this skill, it's yours forever. Start small. Take a class, or a buy a book and practice on little 12″ × 12″ quilt sandwiches. There are many books by expert quilters that teach skills specifically related to this kind of quilting. Two examples are *Machine Quilting with Alex Anderson* and *Foolproof Machine Quilting* by Mary Mashuta, both available from C&T Publishing. Just have fun, and practice, practice, practice!

INSPIRATION

Where do you work? Where do you live? What do you see every day that inspires you? Downtown Houston, with its high-rise buildings, parks, outdoor art, shops, and neighborhoods inspires me. I also love the countryside near Houston—the trees, the water, all that surrounds the city. These are my surroundings, and this is what inspires me daily. I'm sure that if I lived in a small town or by the ocean with different views and vistas, those would be my source of inspiration.

Use what you have and what you know; be inspired by what is around you. There is no right or wrong; you are the best judge of what you love. Keep a notebook, journal, or digital camera with you to capture those inspiring moments. I am constantly surprised at how often I see something new, even when I've passed a place a thousand times. Much of inspiration is being aware and looking for beauty in all that you see.

Photo by Ashlee House

Translating inspiration into a quilt

The next time you see something wonderful and inspirational, think about how you would translate what you see into a quilt. By extracting and reducing your subject matter to its most essential elements, you can re-create its feeling and essence. These quilts are a form of abstraction, not a literal translation. Essential elements of a view or an object can be re-created through the choice of fabric, color, texture, thread, and quilting. For example, *City Sweets* (page 91) is inspired by rows of beautiful pastel-frosted petit fours I've seen in pastry shop windows. The quilt doesn't feature any recognizable images of decadent desserts—but you could get a cavity from the sweetness of the fabric colors!

REFLECTIONS OF YOU

Let your quilts be a reflection of you and your sensibilities, whatever they may be. You may be a minimalist, or you may think that "more is more." Like me, you may think you can never have enough color in a quilt. Let your unique self be reflected in your quilts.

Recently I was having an internal struggle about some fabric that I had ordered. With its gold lines and rich colors, the fabric was beautiful— ornate, and almost decadent in its opulence.

On being inspired
by Ashlee House

As a normal person, that is to suggest, a living, breathing, dreaming person, one who is disappointed with the dregs of life as often as he or she is lifted up by the beauty of it, inspiration and its sources are ever present.

I believe that art is our connection to and proof of a more enlightened being within us. For me it comes like lightning, a window that appears just as quickly as it's gone. But because each of us is so unique, the way inspiration comes to us will vary greatly from one person to the next. After we recognize what that experience is, it is the channeling of that moment that truly defines and teaches who we are as artists.

A book that I have found to be helpful in regard to finding inspiration is *Art & Fear: Observations on the Perils (and Rewards) of Artmaking* by David Bayles and Ted Orland.

CHERRI'S NOTE: My daughter Ashlee is a singer/ songwriter with an amazing ability to craft thoughts, ideals, and feelings into verse. I asked if she would share some thoughts on the creative process.

Detail of *Florin* (full quilt on page 13)

I spent hours poring over quilt books and magazines trying to find inspiration for using this beautiful fabric. For the life of me I couldn't decide on a block or a pattern. Why was I having so much trouble? For a time I put the fabric away on a shelf so that I would see it but not fuss over it. Finally, it came to me that I was trying to create a quilt that was too complicated, with too many pieces. It wasn't my style, and that didn't play to my strengths. When I decided to stop forcing the issue and work with what I knew and was best at, all the difficulties fell to the wayside, and the quilt practically designed itself. To see *Florin,* the quilt that I eventually created using this fabulous fabric, see page 13.

What comes first, the name or the design?

Depends on the quilt! This City Series began with a quilt named *Cityscapes* and has grown to include numerous City quilts. Some of my quilt designs start with the name, and some are the other way around.

Cityscapes, 72½˝ × 77½˝, made and machine quilted by Cherri House

My quilts always tell a story—about myself, the recipient, the fabric, or the subject of the quilt. The quilt name, the fabrics (even the fabric on the back), the colors, and the quilting patterns all add layers of depth and meaning. *Every* quilt has a story, and each decision that you make along the way will help define your quilts as uniquely your own.

I believe that as artists, we need to push ourselves to stretch and grow, but we also need to recognize what we do best, what we are comfortable with, and what fills us with joy to create.

Art and quilting
by Lizzy House

I was talking with a craft store manager about International Quilt Market in Houston, telling her what a neat experience it was to view the show of prize-winning quilts, because it was like being in a museum or a gallery. She said, "I just can't imagine all the time and money and effort that go into those quilts for display. Don't get me wrong, they're beautiful, but they don't serve a purpose." She continued, "Here, we make quilts that serve a purpose—they keep people warm." I replied, "Shouldn't a quilt do both? And don't those quilts in the show serve just as much of a purpose by being beautiful? Does art not have a purpose?"

My mother's City Quilts exemplify the marriage of form and function. They are warm and usable, and they are pieced like any other quilt. But special attention has been paid to the whole design. If you view each of her quilts like a large canvas, you see that each piece in the "exhibition" is an abstract view of an element of the city. The solid fabrics are her artist's palette, and the city is her muse. The city is the source of my mother's inspiration, but yours can be anything—the tree in your front yard, your cat, your trip to Amsterdam.

Quiltmaking can be elevated to new levels of craftsmanship, beauty, and concept by stepping away from the individual block and viewing the whole. As you create your own quilt, view it like a large canvas. How is the composition? How is the contrast? Are there value issues—can you solve them? How is the color? Can you simplify, or edit, the whole?

continued

Remember this: Simplify. To see how a quilt with simple shapes (squares, rectangles, triangles) relates to art, look no further than the likes of good ol' Picasso, Paul Klee, or Piet Mondrian. They simplified shapes and figures and created stunning paintings. In my opinion, they and others, such as mid-century graphic designers, paved the way for the likes of us to create works in a similar, simple way, but with fabric. If you remember to simplify, you don't have to be a champion draftsman or have a master of fine arts degree to be an artist.

Quilts made strictly for warmth and comfort are all right by me, but I believe that they can be both functional *and* beautiful.

NEWS FLASH: This just in. You're an artist.

CHERRI'S NOTE: My daughter Lizzy is a printmaker and fabric designer. She comes to quilting from the unique perspective of an artist who has grown up in a quilting household. I asked her to share her thoughts on art and quilting, and how the two come together.

The Quilts

Take a city tour through twelve textile interpretations using solid fabrics, and explore the many possibilities that can be achieved through this painterly fabric medium. All of the quilt projects that follow are inspired by views in and around the city. These quilts are simple geometric designs cut from strips into squares and rectangles. Basic quiltmaking instructions and information about tools and materials can be found in Cherri's Basics (pages 57, 73, and 83), as well as in Quiltmaking Essentials (page 103).

Note: Specific Robert Kaufman fabric colors are noted only when vital to the overall effect of the quilt.

Each day, as thousands of commuters—myself included—drive in the early morning darkness into downtown Houston, the buildings, lit from within, are a welcome greeting.

In this quilt the blocks—black, alternating with mainly pastels—are the lighted windows of the building. I've used color to create windows where some lights are out and where some are dimmed. Place the medium pastels and the charcoals randomly throughout the black units to give depth and variety to your office building.

City Lights

FINISHED BLOCK | 7″ × 21″

FINISHED QUILT | 65″ × 73″

Machine pieced and quilted
by Cherri House

MATERIALS

- 3¾ yards of black fabric for pieced blocks, sashing, and binding

- 1¾ yards of fabric in a variety of pale pastels for the blocks

- ⅛ yard of each fabric in at least 3 medium pastels for the blocks

- ⅛ yard of charcoal gray fabric for the blocks

- 4⅛ yards of fabric for the backing

- 73″ × 81″ piece of batting

CUTTING INSTRUCTIONS

From the black fabric

Cut 10 strips 7½″ × width of fabric; subcut into 3½″ × 7½″ rectangles for a total of 108 rectangles.

Cut 17 strips 1½″ × width of fabric.

Cut 8 strips 2¼″ × width of fabric.

From the pale pastel fabrics

Cut 14 strips 3½″ × width of fabric; subcut into 3½″ × 7½″ rectangles for a total of 70 rectangles; subcut 8 of these rectangles (in various colors) into 2 strips 1½″ × 7½″, for a total of 16 strips.

From the medium pastel fabrics

Cut 3 strips 3½″ × width of fabric; subcut into 15 rectangles 3½″ × 7½″; subcut 1 of these rectangles into 2 strips 1½″ × 7½″.

From the charcoal gray fabric

Cut 1 strip 3½″ × width of fabric; subcut into 5 rectangles 3½″ × 7½″.

BLOCK ASSEMBLY

Each block contains 4 black rectangles 3½″ × 7½″ and 3 pastel (and an occasional charcoal gray) rectangles 3½″ × 7½″. There are 27 blocks in this quilt.

Refer to the quilt diagram. To give some perspective and color balance throughout the entire quilt, it is recommended that you use a design wall or the floor to arrange the fabric pieces before sewing the blocks. To make each block, sew 4 black 3½″ × 7½″ rectangles and 3 pastel 3½″ × 7½″ rectangles together as shown. Use a charcoal gray rectangle in place of a pastel piece in 5 blocks. Sew a total of 27 blocks, and press all seams toward the black fabric.

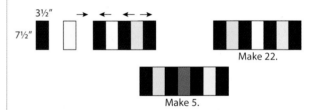

Make 22.

Make 5.

QUILT CONSTRUCTION

This quilt has 9 rows with sashing strips between the rows.

1. Refer to the quilt diagram to arrange the prepared blocks on a design wall or the floor, in a configuration of 3 blocks in a row across and 9 rows down. Think of the blocks creating 3 vertical columns of "windows" in a building. Rearrange if necessary to evenly distribute the blocks with the medium pastels and darkened "windows." Place pastel 1½″ × 7½″ sashing strips between the blocks in each row, again referring to the quilt diagram.

2. Sew each of the 9 rows together, and press the seams toward the black fabric. Return the rows to the design wall in their original location, leaving about 3″ between each row.

Make 9.

3. Use the black 1½″ strips to make 10 sashing strips, 1½″ × 65½″, sewing the strips together and trimming as needed. Place a sashing strip between each row on the design wall and a sashing strip at the top and bottom of the quilt.

4. To ensure alignment of the window units, pin each row and sashing strip from the outer edge of the row first, then pin at the center, and then at multiple spaces in between. Check that the "windows" are all in line before sewing the rows. As you sew the rows and sashing strips together, have the sashing strip against the feed dogs of your machine. Make sure that as you sew over the seam allowances they stay flat (see Sewing over Seam Allowances, see page 106). Press the seams toward the sashing strips.

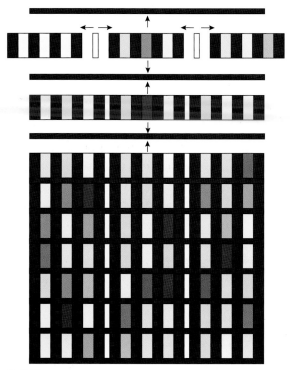

Quilt Diagram

Refer to Finishing Basics (page 107) for information on layering, quilting, and binding your quilt. Use the black 2¼″ strips for the binding.

Lake Houston is a migratory stop for waterfowl in southeast Texas. The lake is a short walk from my backyard. During migration season, when the Canada Geese return, I can hear them honking. Since there are so many birds, I thought they needed their own aviation department. So *City Aviation* was born, complete with Flying Geese blocks and Pinwheel blocks that remind me of airplane propellers!

In fact, this entire quilt is composed of very basic, traditional quilt blocks, including the most basic, the Four Patch and the Log Cabin, as well as some plain blocks. Upping the ante, though, is the fact that the pinwheels and flying geese are made as three-dimensional blocks. Instead of being pieced the traditional way, they are partially detached from the background, giving them a three-dimensional look. Don't let these put you off—they are simple to create, and you will amaze and dazzle your friends.

City Aviation

FINISHED BLOCK | 9″ × 9″

FINISHED QUILT | 72½″ × 72½″

Machine pieced by Cherri House
and quilted by DeLoa Jones

MATERIALS

- 2½ yards of fabric in a variety of light neutrals for the pieced and plain blocks

- 2½ yards of fabric in a variety of medium neutrals for the pieced and plain blocks

- 2 yards of fabric in a variety of dark neutrals for the blocks and binding

- 6¾ yards of fabric for the backing

- 80″ × 80″ piece of batting

CUTTING INSTRUCTIONS

For this project, cutting instructions for the Pinwheel, Flying Geese, Four Patch, and Log Cabin blocks are given in each block section.

From a variety of light, medium, and dark fabrics
Cut 28 squares 9½″ × 9½″.

From the dark fabric
Cut 8 strips 2¼″ × width of fabric.

Layers for 3D unit

BLOCK ASSEMBLY

This quilt contains 9 Pinwheel blocks and 11 Flying Geese blocks, all 3D; and 8 Four Patch blocks, 8 Log Cabin blocks, and 28 plain blocks, for a total of 64 blocks.

basic 3D block unit assembly

The basic construction process for the 3D unit is the same for the Pinwheel and Flying Geese blocks.

1. Position the 2 matching 2¾″ squares right sides together. Fold the contrasting 2¾″ × 5″ rectangle in half with wrong sides together. Insert the folded rectangle between the squares, with the folded edge of the rectangle ¼″ up from the bottom edges of the squares as shown. Match the raw edge sides of the folded rectangle to the raw edges of the squares. Sew along the right side of the layered sandwich.

2. Open the squares. Bring the fold of the rectangle so that it unfolds on the sewn seamline. The unfolded rectangle now forms a triangle on top of the joined squares. Press the raw edge of the opened rectangle so it is even with the top edges of the opened squares. Press the seams open. As this unit is sewn into a block, the top edge of the 3D unit will be in the seam allowance, and the sides of the triangle will be free.

Unfold center.

Press.

Free triangle sides

pinwheel block
Make 9 blocks.

For *each* Pinwheel block

From 1 light or medium fabric, cut 4 rectangles 2¾″ × 5″ and 8 squares 2¾″ × 2¾″.

From 1 contrasting fabric, cut 4 rectangles 2¾″ × 5″.

1. Create 4 units as described in Basic 3D Block Unit Assembly (previous page).

2. Sew a matching background 2¾″ × 5″ piece to each 3D unit as shown. Press the seam allowances as shown.

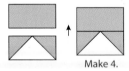
Make 4.

3. Sew the units together in pairs as shown. Press the seam allowances open. Complete the block by sewing the sections together as shown. Again, press the seam allowances as shown.

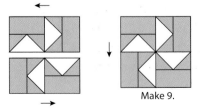
Make 9.

flying geese block
Make 11 blocks.

For *each* Flying Geese block

From 1 light or medium fabric, cut 2 squares 5″ × 5″ and 8 squares 2¾″ × 2¾″.

From 1 contrasting fabric, cut 4 rectangles 2¾″ × 5″.

1. Create 4 units as described in Basic 3D Block Unit Assembly (previous page).

2. Sew the 3D units together in pairs, and then sew each pair to a 5″ square as shown. Press the seam allowances as shown. Complete the block by sewing the sections together as shown.

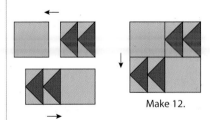
Make 12.

four patch block

Make 8 blocks.

For *each* Four Patch block

From 1 light, medium, or dark fabric,
cut 2 squares 5″ × 5″.

From 1 contrasting fabric, cut 2 squares 5″ × 5″.

Sew the contrasting squares together in pairs.
Press the seam allowances toward the darker
fabric. Then sew the units together as shown.

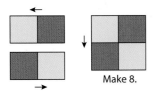

Make 8.

log cabin block

Make 8 blocks.

For *each* Log Cabin block

From 1 light, medium, or dark fabric,
cut 2 rectangles 3½″ × 9½″ and 2 squares
3½″ × 3½″.

From 1 contrasting fabric, cut 1 square 3½″ × 3½″.

Sew the center section together as shown; press
the seam allowances toward the darker fabric.
Then sew the 3½″ × 9½″ rectangles to the top
and bottom of the center section, and press the
seam allowances toward the outside.

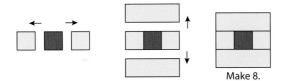

Make 8.

QUILT CONSTRUCTION

This quilt has 8 rows of 8 blocks each.

1. On a design wall, arrange the pieced and
plain blocks into 8 rows of 8 blocks as shown in
the quilt diagram, or in whatever layout you like.

2. Sew each row together, pressing the seam
allowances in opposite directions from row to
row. Join the rows together.

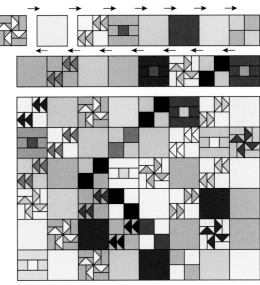

Quilt Diagram

Refer to Finishing Basics (page 107) for information on layering, quilting, and binding your quilt.
Use the dark 2¼″ strips for the binding.

I imagine this is how downtown Houston might appear from a helicopter—*if* the buildings and courtyards were the colors of an Amish quilt. The block is a classic Log Cabin set on the diagonal (on point), with black and navy blue setting triangles used to "float" the blocks.

City Center

FINISHED BLOCK | 11″ × 11″

FINISHED QUILT | 55½″ × 71″

Machine pieced by Cherri House and
machine quilted by DeLoa Jones

MATERIALS

- 3 yards of black fabric for the blocks, setting and corner triangles, borders, and binding

- 2¾ yards total of a variety of light to medium cool-color fabrics (page 20) for the blocks (I used 13 colors in addition to the medium blue for the inner border.)

- ¾ yard of navy blue fabric for the setting triangles

- ⅝ yard of medium blue fabric for the blocks and the inner border

- ⅓ yard of dark gray fabric for the blocks

- 3½ yards of fabric for the backing

- 63″ × 79″ piece of batting

Special equipment

- Spray starch or sizing

- Fons & Porter Easy Diagonal Sets Ruler (optional; see Cherri's Basics: Tools and Supplies, page 57)

CUTTING INSTRUCTIONS

From the black fabric

Cut 4 corner triangles and 6 setting triangles using your preferred method below. Spray the fabric with spray starch or sizing before cutting to prevent stretching the fabric.

Traditional method:
For the 6 setting triangles, cut 2 squares 16⅞″ × 16⅞″; cut diagonally twice for a total of 8 triangles (2 extra).

For the corner triangles, cut 2 squares 8¾″ × 8¾″; cut diagonally once for a total of 4 triangles.

Fons & Porter Easy Diagonal Sets Ruler method:
Follow the manufacturer's instructions to cut 4 corner and 6 setting triangles for a finished 11″ block.

Cut 8 strips 3½″ × width of fabric; subcut 1 strip into 4 squares 3½″ × 3½″.

Cut 8 strips 2½″ × width of fabric; subcut into 28 rectangles 2½″ × 7½″ and 28 rectangles 2½″ × 3½″.

Cut 7 strips 2¼″ × width of fabric.

From the dark gray fabric

Cut 3 strips 2½″ × width of fabric; subcut into 8 rectangles 2½″ × 7½″ and 8 rectangles 2½″ × 3½″.

From the medium blue fabric

Cut 1 strip 3½″ × width of fabric; subcut 2 squares 3½″ × 3½″.

Cut 2 strips 2½″ × width of fabric; subcut into 4 rectangles 2½″ × 11½″ and 4 rectangles 2½″ × 7½″.

Cut 6 strips 1½″ × width of fabric.

From the cool-color fabrics

Cut 1 square 3½″ × 3½″ from each of 12 fabrics.

From each fabric used, cut 1 strip 2½″ × width of fabric; subcut into 2 rectangles 2½″ × 11½″ and 2 rectangles 2½″ × 7½″.

Cut 4 strips 2½″ × width of fabric; subcut into 2 rectangles 2½″ × 11½″ and 2 rectangles 2½″ × 7½″.

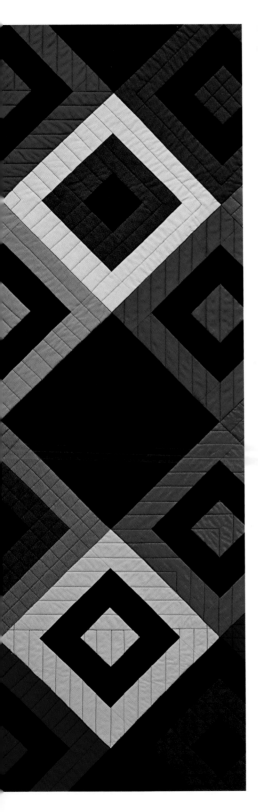

From the navy blue fabric

Cut 4 setting triangles as for the black setting triangles, using your preferred method. Spray the fabric with spray starch or sizing before cutting.

> *Traditional method:*
> For the 4 setting triangles, cut 1 square 16⅞″ × 16⅞″; cut diagonally twice for a total of 4 triangles.

> *Fons & Porter Easy Diagonal Sets Ruler method:*
> Follow the manufacturer's instructions to cut 4 setting triangles for a finished 11″ block.

BLOCK ASSEMBLY

There are 18 blocks in this quilt. Mix and match fabrics to construct each block using whatever combinations you like.

1. Start by sewing a medium blue 3½″ square between 2 black 2½″ × 3½″ pieces.

Add a black 2½″ × 7½″ piece to the top and bottom. Add a medium blue 2½″ × 7½″ piece to the sides. Add a medium blue 2½″ × 11½″ piece to the top and bottom. Press all seams in this block away from the center. Repeat to make a second medium blue Log Cabin block.

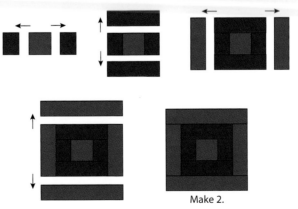

Make 2.

2. Make 12 Log Cabin blocks with a color of your choice in the center and outer rings and a black middle ring.

3. Make 4 Log Cabin blocks using a black 3½″ square as the center, surrounded by a dark gray ring, and then the color of your choice as the outer ring. You now have a total of 18 Log Cabin blocks.

Quilt Diagram

QUILT CONSTRUCTION

The blocks are arranged in 6 diagonal rows.

1. Refer to the quilt diagram, and arrange your blocks on point, 3 blocks across and 4 blocks down, on a design wall. Add the corner and side setting triangles, noting the placement of the dark blue triangles.

2. When you are pleased with your color arrangement, sew the blocks together in diagonal rows, adding the setting triangles to each row. Press the seams in alternate directions from row to row. Return the rows to the design wall.

3. Sew the diagonal rows together, and add the corner triangles last.

BORDERS

For general instructions on adding borders, see Borders (page 108). Use the medium blue 1½″ strips for the inner border and the black 3½″ strips for the outside border.

Refer to Finishing Basics (page 107) for information on layering, quilting, and binding your quilt. Use the black 2¼″ strips for the binding.

Block orientation

To reduce the number of seams to be matched, alternate the orientation of the block for every block—seams vertical, seams horizontal, seams vertical, and so forth.

Basic supplies

Cherri's Basics: Tools and Supplies

You can make all the quilts in this book with basic quiltmaking supplies, most of which are sold at quilt and fabric shops. Here's my list of favorites:

A WELL-MAINTAINED SEWING MACHINE I use the Bernina Aurora 440. But a quality machine need not be fancy or overly expensive. I strongly recommend a refurbished older machine rather than a new plastic one from a discount store.

MACHINE FEET A quilter's ¼″ presser foot is essential for sewing accurate seams (page 106). If you want to machine quilt, see Cherri's Basics: About Quilting (page 83) to read about specialized quilting feet.

SEWING MACHINE NEEDLES My favorites are Schmetz Microtex Sharp Needles. Use good-quality needles, matching the right needle to your thread. Most manufacturers' websites have guidelines for needle or thread requirements. Change your needle after every 8 hours of sewing; it really makes a difference.

ROTARY CUTTERS These are available with 28mm, 45mm, and 60mm blades. I use the Olfa Deluxe 60mm, which has an ergonomic handle and dual-action safety lock, and cuts through multiple layers of fabric. Good for both left- and right-handed users (I'm a lefty).

ROTARY CUTTING RULERS I recommend the Omnigrid rulers in four essential sizes: 6½″ × 24″ for cutting long lengths of fabric and strips; 4″ × 14″ for subcutting strips; and 6½″ × 6½″ and 9½″ × 9½″ squares for squaring up blocks.

FONS & PORTER EASY DIAGONAL SETS RULER This tool allows you to cut both the corner and setting triangles from the same size fabric strip. It's optional for use in *City Center* (page 53) and *City Circle* (page 59). If you wish to purchase one, see Resources (page 110).

GRIDDED ROTARY CUTTING MAT This is wonderful for lining up fabric and rulers to ensure accurate cuts. I find that the Olfa 24″ × 36″ size mat is perfect for my workspace.

SCISSORS There are so many choices! I prefer Fiskars Softouch Scissors in two sizes: the No. 8 Razor Edged Softouch and the Softouch Micro-Tip scissors.

SEAM RIPPER Get a good one—the sharper the better. We all need this tool!

CHALK MARKERS I use these for marking diagonal lines (page 33) and quilting lines.

Some additional, unorthodox supplies that I love include **BLUE PAINTER'S TAPE**, which is great for marking cutting lines on rotary cutting rulers and for marking quilting lines on quilt tops. I also use it to safely wrap up broken sewing needles and used rotary cutting blades.

I use **STICKY NOTES** to stay organized (they even stick to fabric); **INDEX CARDS** to note measurements, numbers of pieces, and so forth, and to tape fabric swatches on; a **DIGITAL CAMERA** to photograph fabrics I'm auditioning on my design wall; and a **CALCULATOR**, because math is a big part of quilting!

The Houston road system has three different circular loops: an inner loop and two additional concentric circles that encompass the city and surrounding areas. Circles and roads—they inspired this traffic quilt!

There are many ways to create circles in quilting. The block in this quilt is a classic called Shoo Fly. Although not a true circle, it reads as a circle, and the circular quilting helps to emphasize the shape.

This quilt provides an opportunity to play with color value and the illusion of transparency. The colors of the "circles" are affected by the square they lie on. In some blocks, it appears as if the circles are sheer and are being colored by squares underneath them. In other blocks, the

City Circle

FINISHED BLOCK	9˝ × 9˝
FINISHED QUILT	77˝ × 77˝

Machine pieced by Cherri House
and quilted by DeLoa Jones

MATERIALS

- 8 yards of assorted fabrics in light, medium, and dark colors for the quilt blocks (backgrounds and "circles")

- 1¾ yards of espresso brown fabric for the setting and corner triangles and the binding

- 1⅛ yards of tan fabric for the setting and corner triangles

- 7⅛ yards of fabric for the backing

- 85″ × 85″ piece of batting

Special Tools

- Spray starch or sizing

- Fons & Porter Easy Diagonal Sets Ruler (*optional;* see Cherri's Basics: Tools and Supplies, page 57).

CUTTING INSTRUCTIONS

From the espresso brown fabric

Cut 10 setting and 2 corner triangles using your preferred method. Spray the fabric with spray starch or sizing before cutting to prevent stretching the fabric.

Traditional method:

For the setting triangles, cut 3 squares 14″ × 14″. Cut each square diagonally twice for 12 triangles (2 extra).

For the corner triangles, cut 1 square 7¼″ × 7¼″. Cut the square diagonally once to make 2 triangles.

Fons & Porter Easy Diagonal Sets Ruler method:

Follow the manufacturer's instructions to cut 10 setting triangles and 2 corner triangles for a finished 9″ block.

Cut 8 strips 2¼″ × width of fabric.

From the tan fabric

Cut 10 setting triangles and 2 corner triangles exactly as you did for the espresso brown triangles.

From the assorted-color fabrics and the remaining espresso brown and tan fabrics

Cut 27 strips 3½″ × width of fabric; subcut into 305 squares 3½″ × 3½″. Sort them by color to make 61 background sets of 5 matched squares.

Cut 16 strips 10½″ × width of fabric; subcut into 61 rectangles 9½″ × 10½″; subcut each rectangle into 2 strips 3½″ × 9½″ and 2 squares 3½″ × 3½″. Keep the pieces cut from the same rectangle together, making 61 circle sets.

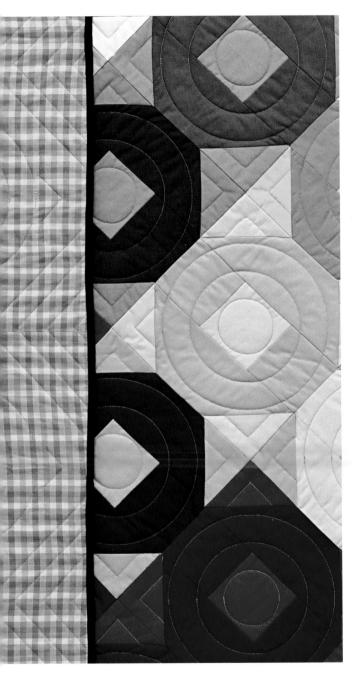

BLOCK ASSEMBLY

This quilt has 61 blocks.

1. Pair up 61 sets of backgrounds and circles to make pleasing color combinations for each block. Working with the pieces for one block at a time, draw a diagonal line from corner to corner on the back of 4 background squares.

2. To make the top and bottom rows of the block, place a background 3½" square on each end of a 3½" × 9½" strip as shown, and sew on the diagonal line of each square. Trim ¼" from the stitching line, and press the triangles and seams toward the corners. Repeat on the second background 3½" × 9½" strip.

Make 2.

3. For the block center row, sew the remaining background square between the 2 "circle" squares. Press the seams to the center. Then sew the strips from Step 2 to the top and bottom of the center as shown. Press the seams to the center.

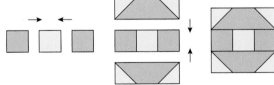

4. Repeat Steps 2 and 3 to complete 61 blocks.

QUILT CONSTRUCTION

The 11 rows in this on-point quilt are diagonal. You will sew the blocks together with setting or corner triangles for each row, and then sew the rows together.

1. Refer to the quilt diagram and arrange your blocks on point, 6 blocks across and 6 blocks down, on a design wall. Note the direction of the seams in each block. Add the corner and side setting triangles, noting the placement of the tan and espresso brown triangles.

2. When you are pleased with your color arrangement, sew the blocks together in diagonal rows, adding the setting triangles to each row. Press the seams in alternate directions from row to row. As you complete each row, return it to the design wall.

3. Sew the diagonal rows together, and add the corner triangles last.

Refer to Finishing Basics (page 107) for information on layering, quilting, and binding your quilt. Use the espresso brown 2¼″ strips for the binding.

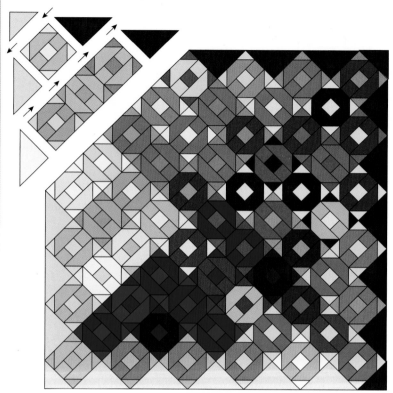

Quilt Diagram

This quilt was inspired by the movie *The Bourne Supremacy*. The inspiration was a building in the background of one scene. As soon as I saw it, I grabbed some paper to try to figure out how to re-create the design. I envisioned a quilt in various greens and blues—like stacks of money. So I decided to call it *City Bank*. What better background for a "money" quilt than black, the color of oil, the lifeblood of Houston!

This quilt has super-simple blocks made from strips, and no border—just a binding.

City Bank

FINISHED BLOCK	10½″ × 10½″
FINISHED QUILT	63½″ × 74″

Machine pieced and quilted
by Cherri House

MATERIALS

- 3¾ yards of black fabric for the quilt blocks and binding

- 2¾ yards of fabric in a variety of green and blue fabrics

- ⅛ yard of lavender fabric for one block

- 4⅝ yards of fabric for the backing

- 71″ × 82″ piece of batting

CUTTING INSTRUCTIONS

From the black fabric

Cut 9 strips 11½″ × width of fabric; subcut into 168 strips 2″ × 11½″ strips.

Cut 8 strips 2¼″ × width of fabric.

From the green and blue fabrics

Cut 41 strips 2″ × width of fabric; subcut into 2″ × 11½″ strips, for a total of 41 sets of 3.

From the lavender fabric

Cut 1 strip 2″ × width of fabric; subcut into 3 strips 2″ × 11½″.

BLOCK ASSEMBLY

This quilt has 42 blocks.

Sew 3 of the same color 2″ × 11½″ strips between 4 black 2″ × 11½″ strips as shown. Press all seams toward the black. Trim the block to an 11″ square.

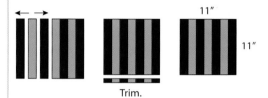

Trim.

QUILT CONSTRUCTION

This quilt has 7 rows of 6 blocks each.

1. Referring to the quilt diagram, arrange the blocks on a design wall with 6 blocks across and 7 rows down. Be sure to place your surprise lavender block where you like it.

2. Sew the blocks into rows, pressing the seams toward the vertical block. (Hint: When sewing the blocks together, sew with the horizontal block on top of the vertical block, and keep the seam allowances flat under the presser foot.) Join the rows together.

Refer to Finishing Basics (page 107) for information on layering, quilting, and binding your quilt. Use the black 2¼″ strips for the binding.

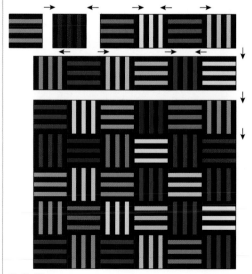

Quilt Diagram

This quilt came about while I was playing with EQ6. I was trying to see what would happen when a simple three-strip block was laid out in an alternating pattern—vertical, horizontal, vertical, horizontal. A herringbone track pattern began to emerge. I chose black for the middle strip, and when I began to change the values of the two side strips, the track pattern became more pronounced. Background and foreground began to pop forward and appear three-dimensional. The addition of varying shades of red, purple, orange, and pink gave the quilt greater depth and sparkle.

The herringbone tracks motif can be found all over the city, from the patterns in men's tweed suits, to those in masonry walls and brickwork, to the patterns of tire tracks. This universal pattern is easily identifiable and very adaptable to a multitude of media.

City Tracks

FINISHED BLOCK	6″ × 6″
FINISHED QUILT	72½″ × 78½″

Machine pieced and quilted
by Cherri House

MATERIALS

- 1¾ yards of black fabric for the blocks and binding

- 3 yards of fabric in a variety of reds for the blocks

- 1 yard of fabric in a variety of purples and pinks for the blocks

- 1 yard of fabric in a variety of oranges and corals for the blocks

- 4⅞ yards of fabric for the backing

- 80″ × 86″ piece of batting

CUTTING INSTRUCTIONS

From the black fabric

Cut 8 strips 2¼″ × width of fabric.

Cut 26 strips 1½″ × width of fabric.

From the variety of colored fabrics

Cut 20 strips 6″ × width of fabric; subcut each strip into 2 strips 4″ × width of fabric and 2″ × width of fabric. Keep the same color strips together.

Cut 6 strips 4″ × width of fabric.*

Cut 6 strips 2″ × width of fabric.*

Pair up a 2″ strip with a 4″ strip, varying in light and dark values.

BLOCK ASSEMBLY

This quilt has 156 blocks.

1. Using a same-color pair of strips, sew a black 1½″ strip between the 4″ and 2″ strips. Press the seams toward the outside. From this strip set, cut 6 blocks 6½″ × 6½″. Repeat to make 19 more same-color strip sets and to cut a total of 120 blocks.

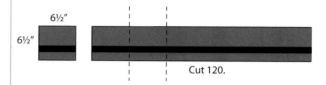

6½″

6½″

Cut 120.

2. Make 6 strip sets with the varying-color pairs and a black 1½″ strip. Cut 36 more 6½″ blocks.

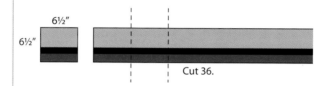

6½″

6½″

Cut 36.

A different view

A reducing glass lens or a door peephole from a hardware store can help you plan placement of the tri-colored blocks by enabling you to see the whole quilt as a smaller image. Look for one at your local quilt shop.

QUILT CONSTRUCTION

This quilt has 12 rows of 13 blocks each.

1. Arrange the quilt blocks on a design wall, alternating the vertical/horizontal orientation of the blocks across the rows and down the columns as shown in the quilt diagram. Approximately 75% of the blocks contain one color plus black. This visually holds the quilt together. The remaining two-color plus black blocks should be randomly distributed throughout the quilt.

2. Sew the blocks into rows, and press the seams in alternate directions from row to row. Then join the rows together.

Refer to Finishing Basics (page 107) for information on layering, quilting, and binding your quilt. Use the black 2¼˝ strips for the binding.

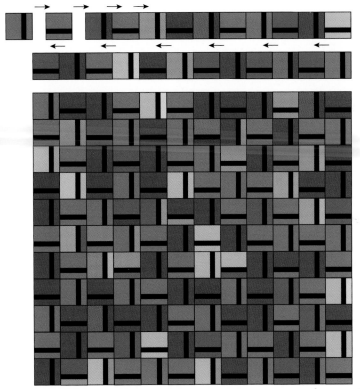

Quilt Diagram

Variety of sewing machine threads

Cherri's Basics: Quiltmaking Materials

THREAD

Choose high-quality thread. There are threads for piecing, threads for the bobbin, and threads for quilting. I am a purist when it comes to piecing: I always use 50-weight, 100% cotton thread.

The type of thread used for quilting can significantly vary the look and texture of your quilt. The weight of thread is determined by a numbering system: The lower the number, the heavier the thread. A 12-weight thread is almost like a very fine yarn, while 100-weight silk thread is extremely thin. Heavier threads almost appear to sit on top of the fabric, whereas thinner threads tend to sink into the fabric.

Before committing to a thread, practice some quilting stitches on a sample quilt sandwich, using the various threads you are considering. Label the threads used, and keep these samples as part of a thread journal for your next quilting adventure. My general preference for quilting is 100% cotton thread in 50-weight, or silk thread in 100-weight, depending on the effect that I am trying to achieve.

BATTING

Battings are available in an array of sizes and lofts, or thicknesses. They can be cotton, polyester, wool, or even bamboo, one of the latest "green" products on the market. I always use Hobbs Heirloom Fusible Batting if I am machine quilting. This batting is 80% cotton and 20% polyester and is fusible on both sides. You simply press the quilt top and back to the fusible batting. When laundered, the fusing product washes away.

FLANNEL BOARD

I'm dyslexic, and I have the hardest time keeping my blocks in order as I move between the design wall and the sewing machine. In order to get my blocks from point A to point B, I made this board.

Flannel board

I wrapped a 16″ × 26″ piece of cardboard in batting, covered it in white flannel, and taped the openings with masking tape. It's not fancy, but it really is my best friend when I need to make a large number of blocks and I absolutely have to keep them in order.

Among the best features of southeast Texas are the trees and all the greenery. Whenever out-of-town guests visit, they are always surprised by how green it is here. Houston is full of parks, both large and small. Memorial Park, with over 1,400 acres that include a densely wooded forest and lots of hiking trails, is literally minutes from downtown. Houstonians don't have to go far to get away!

The colors of *City Green* are the colors you might see on a walk through the woods, with light and shadow playing on the forest floor. On rainy and cloudy days here, the sun seems to backlight the clouds, making the green of the trees especially vibrant. In this quilt, the charcoal sashing and borders function like those clouds, causing the greens to glow.

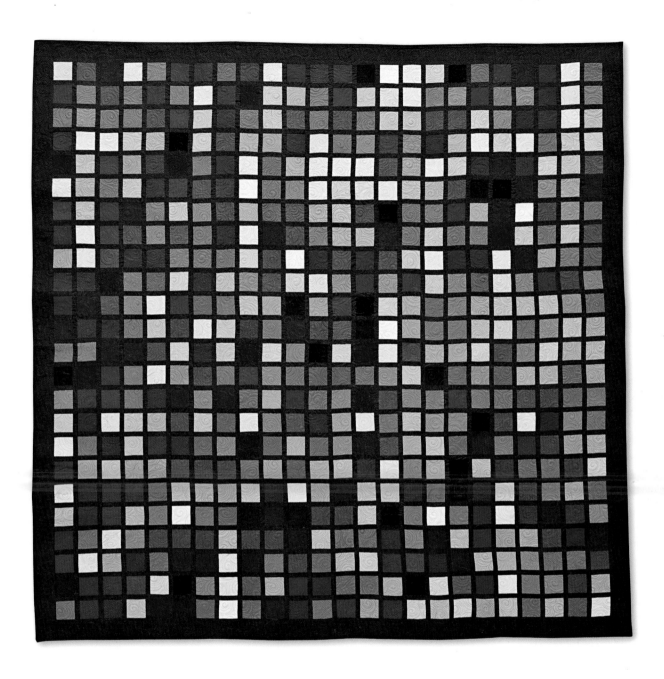

City Green

FINISHED BLOCK | $2'' \times 2''$

FINISHED QUILT | $65'' \times 65''$

Machine pieced and quilted
by Cherri House

MATERIALS

- 2¾ yards of fabric in a variety of greens and blues for blocks

- 3½ yards of charcoal gray fabric for sashing, borders, and binding

- 4⅛ yards of fabric for backing

- 73″ × 73″ piece of batting

CUTTING INSTRUCTIONS

From the assorted green and blue fabrics
Cut 36 strips 2½″ × width of fabric.

From the charcoal gray fabric
Cut 76 strips 1″ × width of fabric.

Cut 7 strips 2½″ × width of fabric.

Cut 7 strips 2¼″ × width of fabric.

UNIT ASSEMBLY

1. Make 36 strip sets by sewing a blue/green 2½″ strip to a gray 1″ strip. Press the seams toward the gray. Cut the strip sets into 576 sections 2½″ × 3″.

2. Sew 6 sections from Step 1 together with the sashing on the left as shown. Press the seams away from the sashing. Make 96 units.

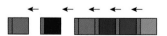

QUILT CONSTRUCTION

This quilt has 24 rows of 4 units each.

1. Refer to the quilt diagram to arrange the quilt rows on a design wall with 4 units in each row as shown. Balance the color throughout the quilt. When you are pleased with your arrangement, sew the units into rows, pressing the seams away from the sashing. Return the rows to the design wall.

2. You will need 25 sashing strips 1″ × 60½″ long. Use the gray 1″ strips to make the sashing. Join the strips together, and trim as needed. You will need 1 sashing strip 1″ × 61″ as well. Set this strip aside until later.

3. Sew a 1″ × 60½″ sashing strip to the top and bottom of the top row. Press the seams toward the sashing.

4. Sew a 1″ × 60½″ sashing strip to the bottom of all the remaining rows. Press the seams toward the sashing. As you sew, have the pieced row against the feed dogs and the sashing on top.

5. Pin the rows at each intersection and sew the rows together. Press the seams toward the sashing.

6. When the rows are together, sew a 1″ × 61″ sashing strip to the right side of the quilt top; press toward the sashing.

BORDERS

For general instructions on adding borders, see Borders (page 108). Use the gray 2½″ strips for the outside border.

Refer to Finishing Basics (page 107) for information on adding borders, layering, quilting, and binding your quilt. Use the gray 2¼″ strips for the binding.

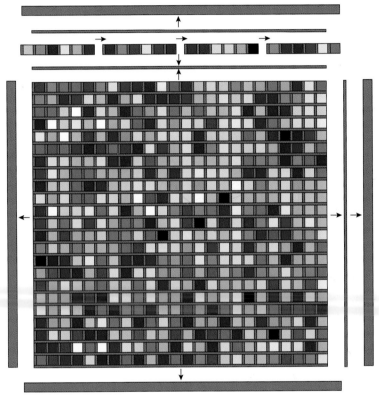

Quilt Diagram

From the Houston Ship Channel to the Gulf of Mexico and all the many lakes and bayous in between, water is an ever-present part of life in southeast Texas. In the harbors and marinas, the narrow shapes of the ships and boats in their slips float on water that reflects the various blues of the sky and the clouds. The simple strip construction of this quilt imitates the pattern of docks, boats, and water.

City Harbor is an exercise in working with closely related color values. I've cited the specific colors of Kona Cotton Solids by Robert Kaufman that I used, because these color values worked so well. Feel free to substitute other fabrics, but be mindful of the value differences

City Harbor

FINISHED STRIP	2¾″ × 71″
FINISHED QUILT	66½″ × 71½″

Machine pieced and quilted
by Cherri House

MATERIALS

- 2¼ yards of black fabric for the quilt strips and binding

- 1 yard of Deep Blue fabric*

- ½ yard of Marine fabric*

- ½ yard of Ocean fabric*

- ⅜ yard of Nightfall fabric*

- ⅜ yard of Pacific fabric*

- ⅜ yard of Teal Blue fabric*

- ⅜ yard of Navy fabric*

- 4¼ yards of fabric for the backing

- 75″ × 79″ piece of batting

*A Robert Kaufman fabric

CUTTING INSTRUCTIONS

From the black fabric

Cut 2 strips 24″ × width of fabric; subcut into 24 strips 3¼″ × 24″.

Cut 8 strips 2¼″ × width of fabric.

From the Deep Blue fabric

Cut 2 strips 14¼″ × width of fabric; subcut into 24 strips 3¼″ × 14¼″.

From the Marine and Ocean fabrics

Cut 1 strip of each color 14¼″ × width of fabric; subcut into 3¼″ × 14¼″ strips, for a total of 12 of each color.

From the Nightfall, Pacific, Teal Blue, and Navy fabrics

Cut 1 strip of each color 10¼″ × width of fabric; subcut into 3¼″ × 10¼″ strips, for a total of 12 of each color.

STRIP ASSEMBLY

This quilt is composed of vertical columns of strips sewn end-to-end. Sew the strips together for each column in the order shown in this chart. (You may want to make a card like this with your fabric swatches.)

Column 1—Make 12.	Column 2—Make 12.
14¼″ Marine	10¼″ Teal Blue
10¼″ Nightfall	24″ Black
14¼″ Deep Blue	14¼″ Ocean
24″ Black	10¼″ Navy
10¼″ Pacific	14¼″ Deep Blue

Stay organized

For your own sanity: As you cut the pieces, label them with the color name to keep them straight. It will help you when you sew the columns.

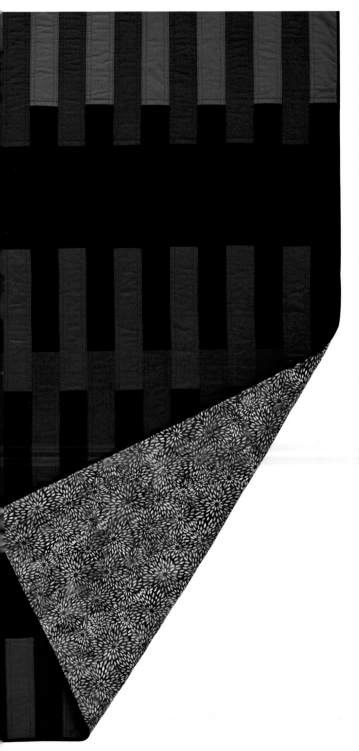

QUILT CONSTRUCTION

Pin the columns together, alternating columns 1 and 2. Pin carefully to ensure that the columns are of equal length before sewing. Sew the columns together; press.

Refer to Finishing Basics (page 107) for information on layering, quilting, and binding your quilt. Use the black 2¼˝ strips for the binding.

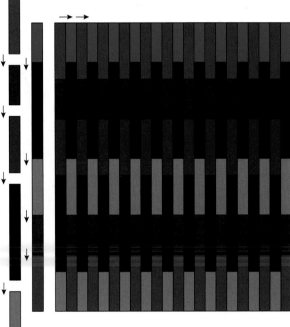

Quilt Diagram

Walking foot and free-motion foot

Cherri's Basics: About Quilting

In addition to being an important part of the quilt design (see Quilting as a Design Element, page 32), quilting holds together the quilt top, batting, and backing. If you want to quilt your creation yourself, you have several options.

TYING is the most basic method of holding the layers together. You simply tie knots, using a needle threaded with embroidery floss, yarn, or narrow ribbon, at evenly spaced intervals all over the quilt. Though simple, it is a perfect solution for some quilts.

HAND QUILTING is a time-honored art. Some quilters consider this the *only* way to quilt a quilt. To learn more about hand quilting, refer to a book like *Hand Quilting with Alex Anderson*, available from C&T Publishing.

MACHINE QUILTING is a skill that can be mastered using a domestic sewing machine, and employing equal amounts of practice and patience. I've used all three types of quilting, but machine quilting is my favorite, and it works best in my busy life.

An alternative to doing your own quilting is to send your quilt top to a professional who uses an industrial-size *longarm* machine. This frees up your time to make more quilts! Plus, a longarm quilter can finish your quilt much more quickly than if you machine quilted it. Longarm quilters normally charge by the inch; prices vary depending on the complexity and originality of the design. To find a good professional, ask at your local quilt shop for recommendations. Ask the quilter for references and samples, as well as for a price and wait-time estimate.

SPECIAL MACHINE FEET FOR QUILTING

A WALKING FOOT is used for utility and straight-line machine quilting. Also called a dual-feed foot, it holds and feeds the quilt layers evenly. Most have an adjustable guide bar that helps you to space your stitching in straight, parallel lines and to create grids. A walking foot is generally sold as an extra accessory to your sewing machine. If you don't have one, check with your machine manufacturer or look in a well-stocked quilt shop.

A FREE-MOTION FOOT (also called an open-toe or darning foot) is the foot to use for decorative free-motion quilting. You drop the feed dogs on your machine, and the needle stays stationary while you move the quilt beneath, as though drawing on your quilt. It takes practice, but it's worth the effort to make unique, creative designs.

For information about threads to use for quilting, see Cherri's Basics: Quiltmaking Materials, page 73.

A massive bridge spans the Houston Ship Channel. Every time I cross the bridge, I can look down on parking lots full of new cars that have just arrived from across the ocean. They're painted in such a wonderful array of bright colors.

Here's a chance to use colors like Tangerine, School Bus, Lime, and Pomegranate! Lots of bright fabrics are united by the brown background and lit up with tiny squares of white.

City Lot

FINISHED BLOCK | 3″ × 6″

FINISHED QUILT | 75½″ × 80½″

Machine pieced by Cherri House
and quilted by DeLoa Jones

MATERIALS

- 4½ yards of chocolate brown fabric for the pieced sashing, border, and binding

- 1 yard of white fabric for the pieced sashing

- 4 yards in a variety of bright fabrics for the blocks

- ½ yard of black fabric for the blocks

- 5 yards of fabric for the backing

- 83″ × 88″ piece of batting

CUTTING INSTRUCTIONS

From the chocolate brown fabric
Cut 18 strips 3″ × width of fabric.

Cut 9 strips 2½″ × width of fabric.

Cut 9 strips 2¼″ × width of fabric.

Cut 19 strips 1½″ × width of fabric; subcut 1 strip into 12 squares 1½″ × 1½″. Put these in a plastic bag, and set aside.

From the white fabric
Cut 18 strips 1½″ × width of fabric.

From the assortment of bright fabrics and the black fabric
Cut 176 rectangles 3½″ × 6½″.

From the black fabric
Cut 2 strips 6½″ × width of fabric; subcut into 22 rectangles 3½″ × 6½″.

SASHING UNIT ASSEMBLY

First, assemble vertical and horizontal strip sets for the sashing.

strip set assembly for vertical sashing

1. Sew a white 1½″ strip between 2 chocolate 3″ strips. Press the seams away from the white. Cut the strip set into 1½″ sections. Make a total of 9 strip sets, and cut a total of 209 sections.

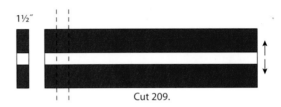

1½″

Cut 209.

2. Set aside 11 sections in the plastic bag with the 12 chocolate brown squares.

strip set assembly for horizontal sashing

1. Sew a white 1½″ strip between a chocolate 1½″ strip and a chocolate 2½″ strip. Press the seams away from the white. Cut the strip set into 1½″ sections. Make a total of 9 strip sets, and cut a total of 216 sections.

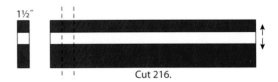

1½″

Cut 216.

2. Set aside 18 sections in the bag with the chocolate brown squares and the 11 vertical sashing sections.

BLOCK ASSEMBLY

Sew a vertical sashing section to a 3½″ × 6½″ rectangle as shown. Press away from the sashing. Then sew a horizontal section to the unit as shown. Press away from the sashing. Double-check for the correct placement of the white patch. Complete 198 blocks.

Make 198.

ADDITIONAL SASHING ASSEMBLY

top sashing row

Refer to the quilt diagram to see the top row of sashing. From your bag of set-aside pieces, sew the 18 horizontal sections together end-to-end as shown. Press the seams away from the chocolate square.

right side vertical sashing

Refer to the quilt diagram to see the vertical sashing row on the right side of the quilt center. From your bag of set-aside pieces, sew the 11 vertical sashing sections between the 12 chocolate 1½″ squares as shown. Press the seams toward the chocolate square.

QUILT CONSTRUCTION

This quilt is assembled in 11 rows of 18 blocks with a top row of sashing added, and then a vertical row of sashing sewn to the right side of the quilt center.

1. Refer to the quilt diagram to arrange the blocks on a design wall in 11 rows across with 18 blocks in each row as shown. Strive for a balance of color across the quilt. The black patches are empty parking spaces, so scatter those throughout the quilt.

2. Sew the blocks into rows. Press the seams in alternating directions. Replace them on the design wall. Then join the rows together, and press.

3. When all the rows are sewn together, refer to the quilt diagram to see the correct positioning for the top sashing row, and sew it to the quilt. Check the placement of the vertical sashing row on the right side, and sew it to the quilt.

BORDERS

For general instructions on adding borders, see Borders (page 108). Use the remaining chocolate brown 1½˝ strips for the border.

Refer to Finishing Basics (page 107) for information on borders, layering, quilting, and binding your quilt. Use the chocolate 2¼˝ strips for the binding.

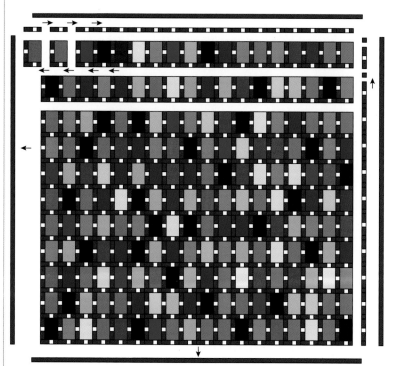

Quilt Diagram

PETIT FOURS! Rows and rows of petit fours with lovely pastel frosting are what I imagined when designing this quilt. On a trip to London, I remember strolling through Harrods Food Halls past beautiful displays of picture-perfect pastries as far as the eye could see. I truly was a "kid in a candy store"! In Houston, my favorite bakery, minutes from downtown, is Andre's—amazing displays, and delicious pastries!

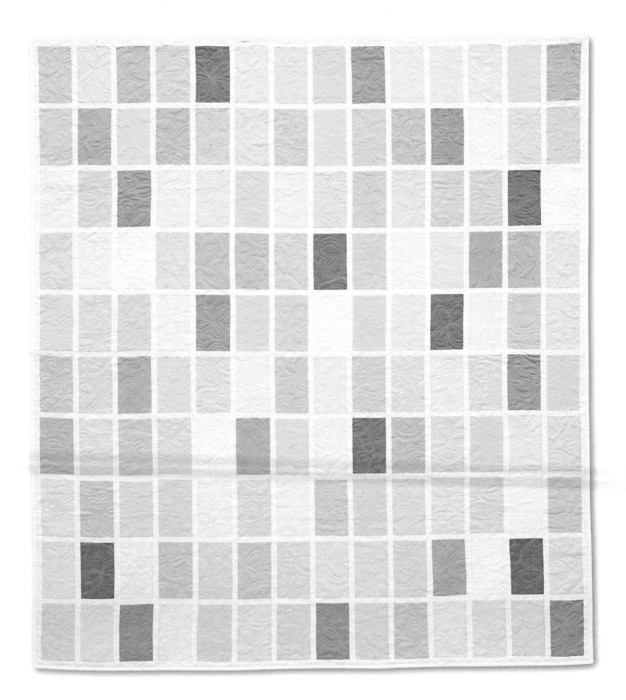

City Sweets

FINISHED BLOCK | 3″ × 5″

FINISHED QUILT | 50″ × 56″

Machine pieced and quilted
by Cherri House

MATERIALS

- 2½ yards of fabric in a variety of pastels for the blocks

- 1¾ yards of white fabric for the sashing and binding

- 3¼ yards of fabric for the backing

- 58″ × 64″ piece of batting

CUTTING INSTRUCTIONS

From the white fabric

Cut 6 strips 2¼″ × width of fabric.

Cut 34 strips 1″ × width of fabric.

From the assorted pastel fabrics

Cut 13 strips 5½″ × width of fabric.

BLOCK ASSEMBLY

This quilt contains 140 blocks.

Sew a 1″ white strip to each of the 13 strips 5½″, and press toward the sashing. Subcut these strip sets into 3½″ units for a total of 140 units.

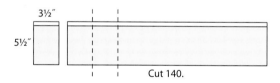

QUILT CONSTRUCTION

1. Refer to the quilt diagram. Arrange the units on a design wall into 14 vertical columns with 10 units in each. Keep the white sashing toward the top of the quilt. Once you are pleased with the color balance, sew each column together, and press the seams toward the sashing. Return the columns to the design wall.

2. Use the remaining 1″ white strips to make 15 sashing strips, 1″ × 55½″, sewing the strips together and trimming as necessary. Make an additional sashing strip 1″ × 50″.

3. Sew the 14 columns between 15 sashing strips. Press all seams toward the sashing.

4. Sew the 1″ × 50″ sashing strip across the bottom of the quilt, and press the seams toward the sashing.

Refer to Finishing Basics (page 107) for information on layering, quilting, and binding your quilt. Use the white 2¼″ strips for the binding.

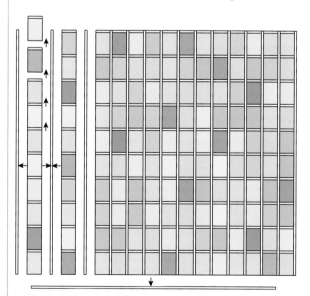

Quilt Diagram

Doesn't every quilter need a quilt about shopping? From Rice Village to Highland Village to Montrose, Houston has terrific neighborhoods and a lot of wonderful stores.

Of course, almost everything we buy these days has a bar code on it. *City Shops* was inspired by the idea of a bar code and, by extension, by great places to shop.

To give this quilt a little more interest, I've taken the liberty of adding a few additional colors (but not too many) to liven up the usual bar code colors of black and white.

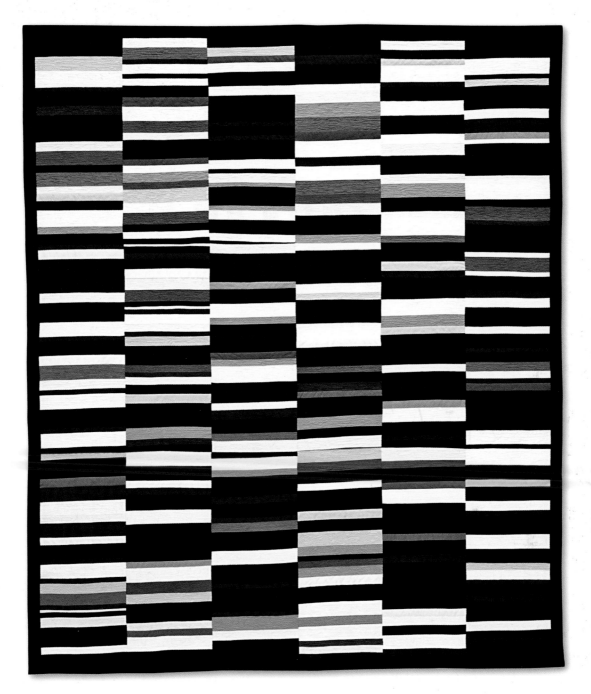

City Shops

FINISHED BLOCK	9½″ × 21½″
FINISHED QUILT	60½″ × 68″

Machine pieced and quilted
by Cherri House

MATERIALS

- 2 yards of black fabric for blocks and binding

- 1⅝ yards of navy fabric for blocks and border

- 1 yard of white fabric for blocks

- 1 yard of light gray fabric for blocks

- ¾ yard of dark charcoal gray fabric for blocks

- ¾ yard of medium blue fabric for blocks

- 3⅞ yards of fabric for backing

- 68″ × 76″ piece of batting

CUTTING INSTRUCTIONS

Cut the binding and border strips first.

From the black
Cut 7 strips 2¼″ × width of fabric.

From the navy
Cut 7 strips 2″ × width of fabric.

From all remaining fabrics
Cut 16 strips 10½″ × width of fabric; subcut into varying widths from ¾″ to 3″ × 10½″.

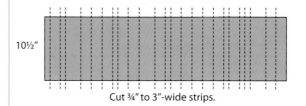

10½″

Cut ¾″ to 3″-wide strips.

BLOCK ASSEMBLY

This quilt has 18 blocks.

1. Sew 2 random 10½″-long strips together along the long edges. Flip the strips open and press the seam to one side. Sew another random strip to the set, flip, and press. Continue adding strips until it is at least 22½″ long. Try to end each 22½″ section with a wide strip so that trimming will be easier.

2. Trim the strip set to measure exactly 10″ × 22″. I found it helpful to fold the strip set in half (folded like a taco) to trim the sides to 10″ wide. Then you can shave off about ¼″ from each side. Repeat these steps to complete a total of 18 blocks.

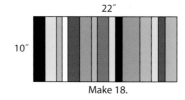

22″

10″

Make 18.

QUILT CONSTRUCTION

1. Refer to the quilt diagram. On a design wall make a pleasing arrangement with 6 vertical columns and 3 blocks down.

2. Sew the columns together; press the seams in alternating directions from column to column. Then join the columns, and press.

BORDERS

For general instructions on adding borders, see Borders (page 108). Use the navy blue 2″ strips for the borders.

Refer to Finishing Basics (page 107) for information on layering, quilting, and binding your quilt. Use the black 2¼″ strips for the binding.

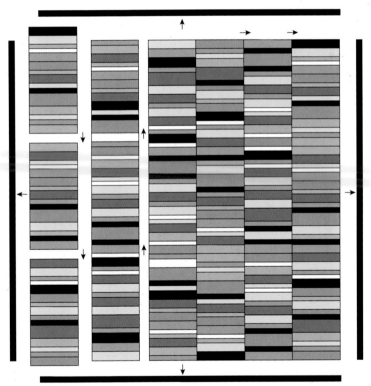

Quilt Diagram

What a life this little quilt has had. It began as a simple Nine Patch and quickly became this riot of color. What better playground for a quilter than to take the most elementary of blocks and turn it on its head by playing with color and value placement? The blocks appear to float, and some of them look as if they are overlapping others. The illusion is created by the use of contrasting color values in the sashing. The foundation of this quilt is as traditional as they come, but by stripping away the traditional configuration, something new and contemporary emerges! Enjoy the evolution of this quilt, and see the possibilities.

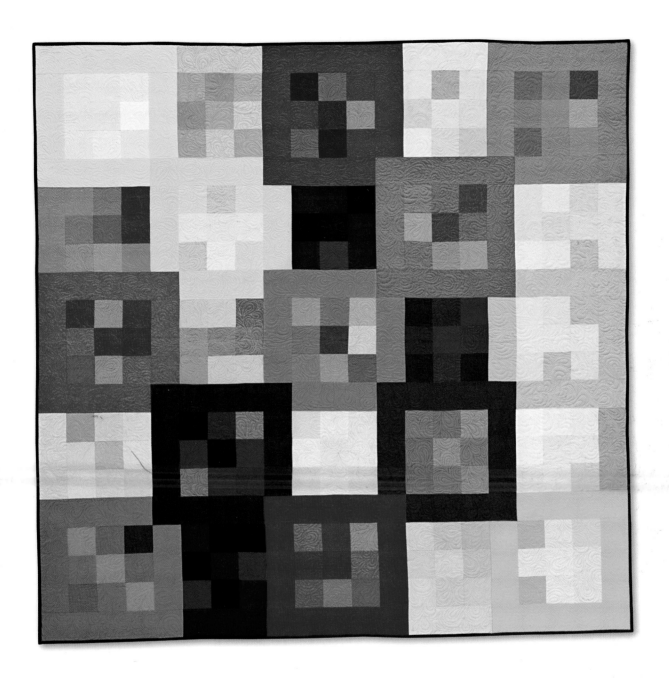

City Play

FINISHED BLOCK | 9″ × 9″

FINISHED QUILT | 63½″ × 63½″

Machine pieced and quilted
by Cherri House

These instructions will serve as a guide, as much as a pattern, for re-creating this quilt. I actually used over 60 color values in my quilt, but you can do the quilt in a more simplified way using fewer color values. To make the "tiles" float and to appear as if they are transparent and lie above or below their neighbors, contrasting values are essential. The placement of varying lengths of the sashing strips produces the illusion of floating. There are three different lengths of 3½″ sashing strips that form the frames for the Nine Patch blocks. Coordinating the cutting of the sashing strips in relationship to each Nine Patch block is essential. Color placement in this quilt is very challenging, but you can accomplish it by following the quilt diagram.

As you experiment to create your own unique version of this quilt, I highly recommend using a design wall, quilting software, or graph paper and colored pencils. You can explore your own color choices and placement.

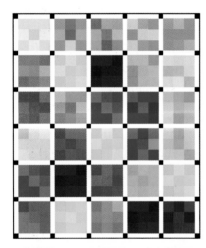

Original Nine Patch with narrow sashing and cornerstones

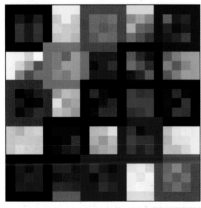

New design in alternate colorway, with sashing width changed

MATERIALS

- 1½ yards of assorted light to dark blues

- 1½ yards of assorted pinks and red-oranges to dark reds

- 1½ yards of assorted light to dark greens

- 1¼ yards of assorted light to dark yellows

- 1 yard of assorted light to dark purples

- ⅝ yard of fabric for the binding

- 4 yards of fabric for the backing

- 72″ × 72″ piece of batting

CUTTING INSTRUCTIONS

From the assorted color groups

Cut 72 blue 3½″ × 3½″ squares.

Cut 54 red 3½″ × 3½″ squares.

Cut 45 green 3½″ × 3½″ squares.

Cut 36 yellow 3½″ × 3½″ squares.

Cut 18 purple 3½″ × 3½″ squares.

From the binding fabric

Cut 7 strips 2¼″ × width of fabric.

Additional cutting will be done in the steps.

BLOCK ASSEMBLY

This quilt has a total of 25 Nine Patch blocks.

1. Arrange a Nine Patch block with assorted 3½″ squares from the same color group. Join the patches into rows, and then join the rows. Follow the pressing arrows. Make 8 blue, 6 red, 5 green, 4 yellow, and 2 purple Nine Patch blocks.

2. Arrange these on the design wall, referring to the quilt diagram for the proper order of colors in each row.

QUILT CONSTRUCTION

All sashing strips are 3½″ wide by various lengths.

1. For the sashing you need to audition 3 yellows (A–C), 5 greens (A–E), 2 purples (A, B), 6 blues (A–F), and 5 reds (A–E). Study the sashings in the quilt photo to see where the light, medium, and dark values are surrounding the various Nine Patch blocks. Once you decide on the specific fabric you want around a specific block, look at the quilt diagram so you can label your colors as yellow A, yellow B, green A, green B, and so on.

2. Using your labels for each fabric, cut the sashing strips for the odd-numbered rows, as indicated in the chart below. These sashing strips are all 3½″ wide by the length indicated in each box.

Row 1	Yellow A 15½″	Green A 9½″	Purple A 15½″	Blue A 9½″	Red A 15½″
Row 3	Yellow A 12½″	Yellow B 12½″	Purple A 12½″	Red B 15½″	Red A 12½″
Row 5	Red D 15½″	Yellow B 9½″	Green B 12½″	Red B 15½″	Green C 12½″
Row 7	Red D 12½″	Blue C 15½″	Green B 9½″	Green D 15½″	Green C 12½″
Row 9	Green E 12½″	Blue C 12½″	Red E 15½″	Green D 12½″	Yellow C 12½″
Row 11	Green E 15½″	Blue E 9½″	Red E 15½″	Blue F 9½″	Yellow C 15½″

3. Using your labels for each fabric, cut the sashing strips for the even rows, as indicated in the chart below. All these sashing strips are 3½″ × 9½″.

Row 2	Yellow A	Yellow A	Purple A	Purple A	Red A	Red A
Row 4	Red C	Yellow B	Yellow B	Red B	Red B	Blue B
Row 6	Red D	Red D	Green B	Green B	Green C	Green C
Row 8	Blue D	Blue C	Blue C	Green D	Green D	Purple B
Row 10	Green E	Green E	Red E	Red E	Yellow C	Yellow C

4. Again using the charts for a reference, arrange the sashing strips around the blocks on your design wall. Sew each row together, and press the seams in alternating directions from row to row. Then join the rows together.

Refer to Finishing Basics (page 107) for information on layering, quilting, and binding your quilt. Use the 2¼″ strips for the binding.

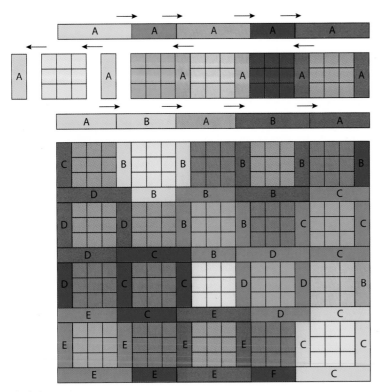

Quilt Diagram

Quiltmaking Essentials

Correct construction and finishing are essential for creating a successful quilt. Here, I offer some of my tips and techniques, along with some finishing basics. (For a listing of my favorite equipment, see Cherri's Basics: Tools and Supplies, page 57.) If you're a beginner, you may also want to consult a good beginning book, such as *Start Quilting with Alex Anderson,* available from C&T Publishing.

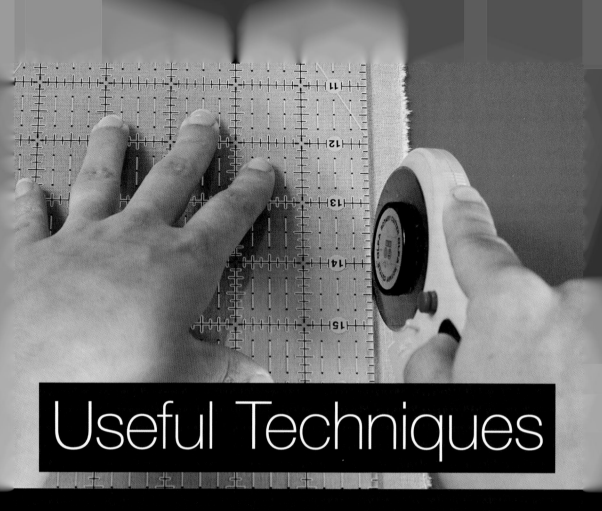

Useful Techniques

Whether you have a dedicated sewing studio or your dining room table does double duty as your sewing space, try to organize it for the numerous steps that you'll follow along the way to making your quilts. If at all possible, have a small ironing tation adjacent to your sewing machine for pressing seams during the block construction phase. To make the most of your quilting time, t is also helpful to have your rotary cutting supplies close by for a seamless (pun intended!) transition between sewing, cutting or trimming, and sewing.

PRESSING

Ironing and pressing are *two different operations.* Ironing is sliding the iron back and forth with gentle pressure to remove wrinkles in the fabric. Pressing is setting the iron down on the area that needs to be pressed in order to set seams. To press long seam lengths, slightly lift the iron and move to the next section, and then press again in the new area.

Iron all of your fabric before cutting. But during the block construction phase, avoid ironing, and use careful pressing techniques instead.

Pressing instructions vary from pattern to pattern; see the individual directions noted in each project. In general, press seams toward the darker fabric to prevent "show-through" from the light side of a quilt block. As you construct each block, press seams in opposing directions, so that when the units are sewn together, the opposing seams will butt or nest. Seams that nest together will require less pinning, less frustration, and flatter seams.

When pressing, always press from the front of the block to prevent tucks in your seams. Quilt row seams should be pressed in alternating directions from row to row in order for the seams to "nest."

Steam or no steam? It's really a matter of personal preference. A common practice among quilters is to use a dry iron during the block construction process, and to use steam to set the block once it is complete.

Finger pressing

During the block construction process, finger pressing is a good alternative to ironing each individual seam. To finger press, use your index finger as an iron, applying gentle pressure along the length of the seam.

Finger pressing

ROTARY CUTTING

Following are some tips for proper rotary cutting:

- Be very careful when working with your rotary cutter; the blade is incredibly sharp. Dispose of dull blades safely.

- Always cut away from yourself.

- Attach sticky dots or sandpaper dots on the underside of your ruler to prevent it from slipping when cutting.

- Where applicable, cut strips first, and then subcut into smaller units.

- To cut strips, fold the fabric selvage to selvage so that both layers of the fabric are flat and are lined up evenly along the selvage edge. Place the fabric fold on the cutting mat grid line closest to you.

For an excellent guide on rotary cutting techniques, see Nancy Johnson-Srebro's *All-in-One Rotary Cutting Magic with Omnigrid* from C&T Publishing.

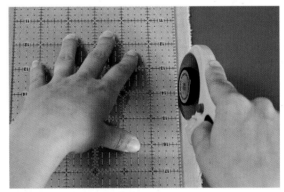

Proper rotary cutting technique

CONSTRUCTION

The standard seam allowance used for quilt construction is ¼˝. Accurate sewing is essential for all of the pieced units to fit together correctly. To begin, you will need a ¼˝ quilter's presser foot for your sewing machine.

Next, test your ¼˝ foot's accuracy. Cut 2 strips of fabric 3˝ × 4˝. Place them right sides together, and put them under the presser foot, aligned with the foot's edge. Sew the length of the strip, and press the seam open.

The finished piece should measure 5½˝ × 4˝. If it doesn't, your ¼˝ foot is not an accurate guide. Place a piece of electrical tape on the throat plate—either just inside the presser foot edge or just outside it, depending on whether your test came out wider or narrower. Repeat the test to ensure that your seam allowances are an actual ¼˝.

PINNING

I am a firm believer in using pins while piecing! Buy super-thin, long pins specifically for piecing. My favorites are Dritz Quilting Crystal Glass Head Pins.

The purpose of pinning is to match seams together and to prevent shifting during sewing. If seams are pressed in alternate directions from row to row, the seams will "nest" together. Pin at every intersection of seams and midway between intersections at approximately every 1½˝–2˝. Insert the pin in the seam approximately ¼˝ in from the raw edge; don't pin through the seam allowance. Check underneath to make sure that the pin is entering the matching seam in the same location.

Place pins like this.

For bulky seams, as in the 3D units in *City Aviation* (page 47) where the seams are pressed open, insert the pin directly in the center of the seam on the top and bottom fabrics.

Don't sew over pins; you can really damage your sewing machine! Remove each pin just before it reaches the sewing needle.

■ ■ Sewing over seam allowances

To ensure that seam allowances stay flat as you sew over them, use the point of a stiletto to hold them down as they approach the presser foot.

Finishing Basics

You have dreamed, planned, purchased, ironed, cut, sewn, pressed, maybe cut again, sewn again, and pressed one last time. You aren't quite finished, though; there are still decisions to be made. As some quilters say, "It's not a quilt till it's quilted." You must layer and baste, then quilt. The final step is binding.

BORDERS

When border strips are cut on the crosswise grain, piece the strips together to achieve the needed lengths.

Note: For quilts without a border, backstitch at the beginning and ending of each row, or sew around the entire perimeter of the quilt ⅛″ from the edge. This will prevent seams from popping open during the handling and quilting of your top.

Squared borders

In most cases the side borders are sewn on first. When you have finished the quilt center, place pins at the centers of all four sides of the quilt. Then measure through the vertical center of the quilt. This will be the length to cut the side borders. Place pins at the centers each border strip. Pin the side borders to the quilt, matching the center pins. Using a ¼″ seam allowance, sew the borders to the quilt and press toward the border.

Measure horizontally across the center of the quilt including the side borders. This will be the length to cut the top and bottom borders. Repeat, pinning, sewing, and pressing.

BACKING

Plan on making the backing a minimum of 8″ longer and wider than the quilt top. Piece, if necessary. Trim the selvages before you piece to the desired size.

To economize, piece the back from any leftover quilting fabrics or blocks in your collection.

BATTING

The type of batting to use is a personal decision (see Resources, Quiltmaking Supplies, page 110). Cut batting approximately 8″ longer and wider than your quilt top. Note that your batting choice will affect how much quilting is necessary for the quilt. Check the manufacturer's instructions to see how far apart the quilting lines can be.

LAYERING

Spread the backing wrong side up and tape the edges down with masking tape. (If you are working on a carpeted floor, you can use T-pins to secure the backing to the carpet.) Center the batting on top, smoothing out any folds. Place the quilt top right side up on top of the batting and backing, making sure it is centered.

BASTING

Basting keeps the quilt "sandwich" layers from shifting while you are quilting.

If you plan to machine quilt, pin-baste the quilt layers together with safety pins placed a minimum of 3″–4″ apart. Begin basting in the center and move toward the edges first in vertical, then horizontal, rows. Try not to pin directly on the intended quilting lines.

If you plan to hand quilt, baste the layers together with thread using a long needle and light-colored thread. Knot one end of the thread. Using stitches approximately the length of the needle, begin in the center and move out toward the edges in vertical and horizontal rows approximately 4″ apart. Add 2 diagonal rows of basting.

QUILTING

Quilting, whether by hand or machine, enhances the design of the quilt. As described in Quilting as a Design Element (page 32), you may choose to quilt in-the-ditch, do straight-line quilting, or do your own free-motion quilting. Remember to check your batting manufacturer's recommendations for how close the quilting lines must be. For more details on quilting, see Cherri's Basics: About Quilting (page 83).

BINDING

Trim excess batting and backing from the quilt even with the edges of the quilt top.

Double-fold straight-grain binding

Cut the binding strips and piece them together with diagonal seams to make a continuous binding strip. Trim the seam allowance to ¼˝. Press the seams open.

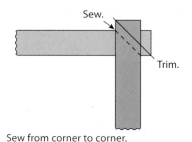

Sew from corner to corner.

Completed diagonal seam

Press the entire strip in half lengthwise with wrong sides together. With raw edges even, pin the binding to the front edge of the quilt a few inches away from the corner, and leave the first few inches of the binding unattached. Start sewing, using a ¼˝ seam allowance.

Stop ¼˝ away from the first corner (see Step 1), and backstitch one stitch. Lift the presser foot and needle. Rotate the quilt one-quarter turn. Fold the binding at a right angle so it extends straight above the quilt and the fold forms a 45° angle in the corner (see Step 2). Then bring the binding strip down even with the edge of the quilt (see Step 3). Begin sewing at the folded edge. Repeat in the same manner at all corners.

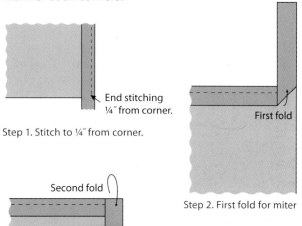

Step 1. Stitch to ¼˝ from corner.

Step 2. First fold for miter

Step 3. Second fold alignment

Continue stitching until you are back near the beginning of the binding strip.

Finishing the binding ends

After stitching around the quilt, fold under the beginning tail of the binding strip ¼˝ so that the raw edge will be inside the binding after it is turned to the backside of the quilt. Place the end tail of the binding strip over the beginning folded end. Continue to attach the binding, and stitch slightly beyond the starting stitches. Trim the excess binding. Fold the binding over the raw edges to the quilt back, and hand stitch, mitering the corners.

Resources

QUILTMAKING SUPPLIES

Aurifil
Threads
www.aurifil.com

Bernina USA
Sewing machines
www.berninausa.com

C&T Publishing
Inchie Ruler Tape
www.ctpub.com

Fiskars
Softouch Scissors
www.fiskarscrafts.com

Fons & Porter
*Fons & Porter Easy Diagonal
Sets Ruler*
www.fonsandporter.com

Hobbs Bonded Fibers
Hobbs Heirloom Fusible Batting
www.hobbsbondedfibers.com

Moleskines.com
Moleskine notebooks
www.moleskines.com

Olfa
*Rotary cutting mats,
rotary cutters*
www.olfa.com

Omnigrid
*Rotary cutting rulers,
rotary cutting mats*
www.dritz.com/brands/
omnigrid/

Robert Kaufman Fabrics
Kona Cotton Solids
www.robertkaufman.com

WonderFil
InvisaFil Thread
www.wonderfil.net

YLI Corporation
Silk thread
www.ylicorp.com

QUILTING SOFTWARE

The Electric Quilt Company
EQ6 Quilt Software
www.electricquilt.com

REFERENCES

Gee's Bend Quilts:
www.quiltsofgeesbend.com

http://www.auburn.edu/
academic/other/geesbend/
explore/catalog/slideshow/
index.htm

http://www.
allianceforamericanquilts.org/
projects/quiltsofgeesbend.php

Arnett, Paul, William Arnett, Bernard Harman, et al. *Gee's Bend: The Architecture of the Quilt.* Atlanta: Tinwood Books, 2006.

Arnett, William, Alvia Wardlaw, Jane Livingston, et al. *The Quilts of Gee's Bend: Masterpieces from a Lost Place.* Atlanta: Tinwood Books, 2002.

Amish Quilts:
www.quiltindex.org > Search > Religious, Ethnic and/or Cultural Affiliation > Amish

Pellman, Rachael. *The World of Amish Quilts.* Intercourse, PA: Good Books, 1969.

About the Author

Photo by Ashlee House

Cherri House is a quilt designer and owner of Cherry House Quilts, along with her daughter Lizzy. Cherri was taught to sew at a very young age by her mother, an accomplished seamstress. Her first conscious memory of a quilt was one made by her grandmother. That humble, made-from-scraps patchwork quilt was, in her eight-year-old heart, the most beautiful thing she had ever seen. This first "real" quilt sparked in her a love of quilting that has never been quenched. Nor has her desire to wrap everyone in a quilt, to keep them warm and loved. She definitely believes the world would be a better place if everyone had a quilt.

Geometric and graphic quilts designed as a whole are Cherri's signature style, which has evolved from her first quilt at age twelve, with her mother. A constant in her quilting adventures is her love of color and fabric—"the more the merrier" is her motto.

Cherri's first love has always been her family. As a single mother to Luke, Elizabeth, Ashlee, and Melissa, quilting often took a back seat to rearing her family. But it has always been a source of comfort during stressful times. In 2007, within two weeks of her last "little one" leaving home, Cherry House Quilts was born—a long-awaited dream came true!

Cherri lives in Humble, Texas, with her noble pup Mickey, "king of no races," and her three cats, Pinecone, Stella, and Finn.

Cherri's website: www.cherryhousequilts.com

For a list of other fine books from C&T Publishing, ask for a free catalog:

C&T PUBLISHING, INC.

P.O. Box 1456
Lafayette, CA 94549
800-284-1114

Email: ctinfo@ctpub.com
Website: www.ctpub.com

C&T Publishing's professional photography services are now available to the public.
Visit us at www.ctmediaservices.com.

Tips and Techniques can be found at www.ctpub.com > Consumer Resources > Quiltmaking Basics: Tips & Techniques for Quiltmaking & More

For quilting supplies:

COTTON PATCH

1025 Brown Ave.
Lafayette, CA 94549
Store: 925-284-1177
Mail order: 925-283-7883

Email: CottonPa@aol.com
Website: www.quiltusa.com

Note: Fabrics used in the quilts shown may not be currently available, as fabric manufacturers keep most fabrics in print for only a short time.

stashBOOKS

fabric arts for a handmade lifestyle

If you're craving beautiful authenticity in a time of mass-production...StashBooks is for you. StashBooks is a new line of how-to books celebrating fabric arts for a handmade lifestyle. Backed by C&T Publishing's solid reputation for quality, StashBooks will inspire you with contemporary designs, clear and simple instructions, and engaging photography.

www.stashbooks.com